SALLY Z

Speaking Story

Using the magic of storytelling to make your mark, pitch your ideas, and ignite meaningful change

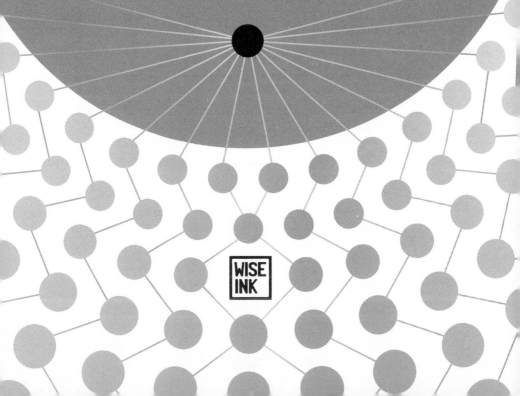

WISE
INK

To protect the confidentiality of clients, I have created characters that are
fictionalized composites based on a compilation of real situations where the
details of the precipitating events have also been combined and altered. Any
similarities between the identifying details of the fictional characters and clients I
have seen are coincidental.

ISBN 13: 978-1-63489-670-2

Library of Congress Catalog Number: 2023917020

Printed in the United States of America
First Printing: 2023
27   26   25   24   23   5   4   3   2   1

Cover design by Luke Bird
Interior design by jamesmonroedesign.com

This book is also available in an electronic version.

Wise Ink, Inc.
wiseink.com
To order, visit www.itascabooks.com or call 1-800-901-3480.
Reseller discounts available.

To my people: Andy, Ro, Luke, and Harps.
It's always all for you.

And to my speakers: for your courage.
You push me to be better.

CONTENTS

PROLOGUE

You belong on stage.

You do. Even if you don't believe it yet.

You have lived experiences. A needed message. A story that your audience is waiting to hear.

And yet, despite the passion and purpose bubbling up inside you, you are hiding, frustrated by unrecognition and forever feeling like you're not enough.

The world has told us that speaking is for the special unicorns who live among the stars. That idea is keeping too many of us from sharing our most daring and needed ideas, owning our stories, and stepping up and out as leaders in a world that desperately needs those ideas and stories.

So we perfect every gesture. Obsess over every word. Stand in the wings of the main stage of our lives. Waiting for some sign that we belong out front, that we are worthy of the moment.

This is your sign.

It's time to dare to move your audience, instead of merely speaking to it. To move beyond the trap of admiration that keeps you in the cage of perfection and procrastination. To take a deep breath and step into the spotlight. *To be seen anyway. To be*

known anyway. To speak anyway. Despite your humanness, your failings, your imperfections, your self-doubt.

You don't have to have written a book or gone through some big life turmoil.

You don't have to be outgoing, confident, beautiful, or the smartest person in the room.

You don't have to be eloquent or polished, or wear a fancy blazer.

You have everything you need. Right now.

If you would only take the risk—and believe in what's possible.

So dare to step out front and speak your story. ***It's how you, and all of us, will inspire a better future.***

Remember this: ***You belong on stage.*** You do. Even if you don't believe it yet.

But I believe it. I believe in you. And I will show you the way.

INTRODUCTION:
TELL THE STORY WITH YOUR WHOLE HEART

The definition of courage is to tell your story with your whole heart.

— BRENÉ BROWN

You should know before I begin this that I'm a pretty (okay, *very*) positive person. I don't generally walk around criticizing or analyzing other people and how they show up in the world. But as an award-winning speaker and speaking coach for the last twenty-plus years, it's an occupational hazard of mine to "always be assessing," or to ABA.

Whether it's a commercial ("That turn of phrase was so on point!"), a church sermon ("Whoa, way too long"), a funeral eulogy ("The vulnerability! And courage!"), a TED Talk ("Interesting, but robotic"), an Instagram Reel ("Hilarious!"), a keynote speech ("Too many points")—I can't help it! I am in the business of constantly assessing whether I was *moved* by something (or whether any "audience" was moved by it) and why, so I can then implement that in my work.

Sitting at a fundraising event a few years back was no different. I was definitely (*ahem*) ABAing.

It was one of those award ceremonies that nonprofits put on to get people together, remind them of their mission, and raise money while they're at it. And I love events! As a former actor, I am drawn into the thrill of what happens (or what may happen) when a bunch of people gather together in a live experience and someone compels an audience to *do* something. It's live theater meets a mission, and that combination is music to my ears and why I love what I do. I have helped run dozens of fundraising events over the years; and if done right, they are truly a thrill—and an incredibly effective way to garner trust, raise money, and inspire needed action.

But that's not always the case.

This particular event was a (frustrating) parade of awards and some awkward transitions, all of which aren't out of the ordinary (and sadly somewhat expected for the average event-goer). What was clear to me was that there was an evident lack of story in this event. Instead, it was a string of the following:

- Talking about themselves

- Talking about their businesses

- Talking about their mission and goals

Which are all fine and good things to talk about. It's critical information. The emcee was doing his best to be entertaining during all the talking, and the audience gave their obligatory applause and appreciation.

It was fine. Not a "Here, take my money" kind of event, but fine. Until one award recipient got up.

As he took the stage and stood in front of the podium, he took a breath. Then, without going into any "thank you so much" standard practice response to getting an award (which we hardly listen to anyway), he started telling a story: "When I was twelve, my dad wrote a letter to the superintendent. . . ."

It was like someone had tipped the audience on its axis toward the stage. We leaned in. The mood shifted. We were listening. And by the end of the story, I knew not only what his work was, but also *why* it mattered.

He took his time. He set the scene. And his story led us perfectly to a point: *When someone believes in you, like his dad did, anything is possible.*

It was poignant and polished. And yes, I cried. (Okay, yes, I do cry at commercials and a surprising number of Instagram Reels. But it wasn't just me crying. My objectively-difficult-to-make-cry husband also teared up.)

I wanted to go home and be a different parent because of it. And I thought, *Here's my credit card! TAKE IT ALL!*

(I should note that we knew this speaker was grateful, even though he didn't explicitly tell us through all the thank-yous immediately after taking the stage.)

That's the power of a story: It gets us out of our heads and into our hearts. It helps the audience not just understand something intellectually, but also feel it.

Stories are the tool of the heart, and the heart is where persuasion happens. Simply put, if you can speak a powerful story, you can lead more effectively—and more meaningfully.

If you take in the ideas from this book and put them to work the next time you step out front, you will not only captivate in those big or small moments. You will also lead, persuade, and influence in ways you didn't know you were capable of before.

Together, in this book, *we are going to help you speak your story so that you, too, can move the world.*

Stories have been the tool of my trade for nearly thirty years. I have spent that time working with CEOs, changemakers, entrepreneurs, and leaders to create talks that will move their audience. It's why I'm here on this earth: to help people bring their voice and their stories out to the world with more authenticity, clarity, and courage.

And it brings me so much joy that you're here, because I believe that stories have a big and needed place in this world—and that includes *your* story.

HOW TO USE THIS BOOK

I'm writing my story so that others might see fragments of themselves.

— LENA WAITHE

This book is set up to do two key things:

1. Equip you with the core ideas you need to understand so you can speak your story

2. Provide you with some tangible tools to actually do it

This book is divided into six parts. Except for part 1, each part is followed by a section called "Sparks." The "Sparks" sections are meant to help you shift these ideas from theory into practice, and they include three elements:

1. A **summary** of the key ideas from its respective part

2. One or two **exercises** you can do right in that moment to help those ideas become more real

3. **Tools** or **resources** you can take with you as you continue to grow and develop

All of these tools and resources in the "Sparks" sections can be found through the QR code below:

In each "Sparks" section, I'll identify which tools apply to that specific part. For example, in part 1, we'll talk about the power of consistency and simply "doing it anyway." So I'll point you toward the #ShowUpAnyway Email Series, which can help you practice this story strategy on the "free stages" to help you move through any discomfort or fear that may be holding you back. You can find the #ShowUpAnyway Email Series, along with all the other tools and resources, using the above QR code.

Most importantly, this book isn't meant to just give you something to think about. Yes, much of your speaking and storytelling success comes from your mind. ***But to convince the mind, we have to do the work.***

I hope this book empowers you to step out front and share yourself with courage!

part 1:

The Foundation:
Stories Are the Tool of the
Revolution (Or Whatever Change
You Want to Make)

chapter 1

Stories Are the Tool

The stories we tell literally make the world. If you want to change the world, then you need to change your story.

—— MICHAEL MARGOLIS

I was standing up in front of about 150 seventh graders. It was as smelly as you might think—and as frustrating and difficult. But it was also so much fun! Seventh graders are the most amazing combination of heartbreaking and uplifting, and I love speaking to them because if you can win their trust, they will go with you 100 percent.

I was speaking for Youth Frontiers, a national youth-serving organization. It was our job to show up and convince an entire class of teenagers to treat one another differently. We talked about big, universal ideas like kindness, courage, and respect in large-group activities, small-group conversations, and two twenty-minute TEDx-style talks. It was a week of camp, all jammed into one day.

That day, I was speaking about courage. As you can imagine, seventh graders are not so into courage. (Although I think it takes a lot of courage to be a seventh grader!) I remember standing at the front of the packed gym, microphone in hand, feeling this sense of disconnect. The students were squirrelly, looking behind me, turning to their neighbors, and being really chatty. I was pouring my heart into these big ideas, and I wanted so badly for them to take in the messages.

But in that moment, it was painfully obvious that they didn't give a crap about courage (yet). They didn't really know what it looks like. They didn't know what impact it could have on their lives. They didn't know why it would ever be worth the risk.

And why should they care? My simply telling them to care is just another adult telling them what to do, without showing them *why* they should do it. (Every parent on the planet eventually learns this hard lesson.) These seventh graders were NOT with me.

So I made a game-time call: I skipped past the next five minutes of what I'd planned to share—which were some seriously powerful one-liners that they weren't going to listen to—and jumped right into a story about John.

John was a student I had met a few weeks back at a different event. He was one of those kids who was so excited to spend the day with us. He came in with so much energy and a positive spirit; and as an adult, I was like, *Oh, what a sweet kid*. I immediately loved him.

But, thanks to the unique perspective I had from the front of the room, I also noticed that John was alone a lot. He sat by himself during lunch. Nobody would sit with him when we gathered in a large group. I had a feeling that John was having a rough time at school and didn't have a lot of friends.

At the end of this retreat experience, we invited the students to walk into the center of the room and share how they're going to act with courage more often in their lives. The first student to get up was John. He walked to the middle of the room, picked up the microphone, looked around at his classmates, and said with a shaking voice, "I hear what you say about me. I want you to know that it hurts. And my act of courage is to ask you to please stop."

And the whole feel of the room changed.

Talk about an act of courage! John's classmates responded in the most beautiful way: by supporting him, making commitments to change, and even being more present with him. It was a remarkable moment that I will never forget. Which is why I decided to share his story with my squirrelly seventh graders.

As I talked about John and his act of courage, *our* whole room changed. The students were quiet and leaning in. I could almost see their brains processing, empathizing, thinking, wondering: *If that was me, would my classmates respond? How would I respond if the John in my class got up and did that?*

I felt this sense of focus and commitment, and I thought, *WOW. Story is so powerful.*

It became clear to me in that moment that story is how we

get those big, beautiful, important ideas into the seventh graders' hearts and minds, even when they are initially resistant. Without story, our messages don't have a chance.

Whatever change *you* want to make—whether it's a new product, a new program, a different way of being, a new policy, an innovation, or a stand you want to take—the revolution or change you want to make needs the tool of story to work.

Take, for example, the rapid pace of change in the realm of LGBTQ+ rights over the last two decades. That change was fueled (very intentionally) by stories. Here in Minnesota, where I grew up and am now raising my own family, there was a proposed ban on gay marriage during the 2012 midterm elections. At the time, I had three young kids, and I felt deep within me that I wanted to protect the rights of my LGBTQ+ friends and family. So one day, between toddler music lessons and story time, I took my littles to the "Say Yes to No" office to grab a yard sign to proudly display my support.

Now, I have strong feelings about things, but I'm also a proud Minnesotan and a do-gooder and people pleaser. And, well, I don't like conflict. I don't love the inherent divides that are created when we publicly say "THIS IS WHAT I BELIEVE" through a sign or button because, of course, humans are more complex and nuanced than what most signs or buttons can fairly communicate. It puts us into distinct camps against one another instead of finding common ground.

But on this issue, I knew I needed to overcome my desire to moderate and people-please in order to protect the LGBTQ+ community. So I grabbed that sign and explained to the kiddos that we would be putting it in our yard because "love is love"; and if two women or two men love each other, they should be able to get married to show their commitment, and the world should understand their commitment to each other as well.

"You know Stephanie and Morgan?" I asked my kids.

"Yes!" (They love our friends Stephanie and Morgan.)

"They love each other and deserve to get married," I said. "Just like me and Daddy."

They got that. Mom and Dad are married, and they love each other. Morgan and Stephanie love each other, so why can't they get married? It's the universal love story of two people wanting to commit their lives to each other—and to have the world recognize and understand their level of commitment.

As we were leaving the office, one of the workers handed us a flier encouraging us to talk to others about why we support stopping the ban. On the flier, they shared their core strategy, and it went something like this:

> Share your stories. Share about the people in your life who are and have been affected by laws like this. Share your values around marriage—and how those values are the same ones that lead heterosexual couples to want to get married.

In other words, it was asking us to tell the love stories of these folks—because underneath the categories and divisions is the SAME story: We met, we fell in love, we longed for a deeper commitment, and we invited the world to recognize that commitment as we build our life together.

Minnesota defeated the ban on gay marriage, thanks in part

to story. That same approach has been used again and again to humanize issues where people stand staunchly in disparate camps. The more stories we tell, the more change that happens. Because once you know the story of Stephanie and Morgan, you recognize your own love story in theirs.

And though that particular story is about love, this is not squishy stuff we're talking about. Stories are at the heart of every idea and human aspiration that has ever existed. Behind the mission to Mars? Story. Behind every fictional and nonfictional writing project? Story. Behind your bold new idea? A story. Stories are the currency of empathy, connection, resonance, and trust. Stories can create (and dissolve) business partnerships, tap into innovation, or alienate and exclude through fear. ***Stories are the tool of the revolution—whatever revolution you're working on.*** Whether your world is 150 seventh graders, a business conference room, or the TEDx stage, your words and stories are what will move it.

chapter 2

Speaking Is Leadership in Action

Storytelling is the most powerful way to put ideas into the world today.

— ROBERT McKEE

There are lots of ways for you to share your stories. Speaking them is only one way. You can write it, draw it, put it in a commercial, write a memoir, or plaster it on your blog. All of those ways are fine and good. But in my opinion, they're not quite as impactful as speaking it. There is something about the particular art of standing up and speaking your story, even virtually.

When I stand onstage to talk about stories, I'm trying to get people to understand something you can only understand when you experience it yourself. You are standing up for an idea—

literally. This is leadership in action. It is the embodiment of your idea, in the human form of your physical presence, your body, your words, your tone, and your actions.

You can't fake it. (Well, you can try, but it won't work very well. We'll see through it.) So it challenges us in a particular way to publicly commit to this idea and story as a part of us. It pulls us out of our anonymity.

If you are speaking your story, it's important to note that it means you are not a writer. (I mean, you may also be a writer. But that's not what we're talking about here.) I want you to shift your thinking from "I am going to write this story" to "I am going to *speak* this story." Watch how that changes you and how you feel about it. There is something about the act of getting up on your feet and saying words out loud that gets your heart pumping in a different way. The risk of vulnerability and speaking puts you on the line in a way that nothing else does: *If I'm going to stand up and say this, I better believe it. It's gotta be in me.* **Because I am literally standing for it.**

And as we do this, we are talking about leadership as much as we're talking about speaking. It's a beautiful parallel development because the risks we take as leaders, entrepreneurs, and changemakers reflect how we show up as speakers—because *speaking is leadership in action.*

So as you bring your message and story out into the world more, it requires leadership to do it well—and to do it with the kind of impact you want to have.

chapter 3
Why Tell Stories?

Stories are a communal currency of humanity.
— Tahir Shah, *In Arabian Nights*

Let's get really specific about why stories are the most important persuasion tool in your leadership tool kit. Because I realize you might be thinking, *What is this magic called persuasion that you keep talking about, Sally?*

After I experienced the persuasive magic of stories as I stood in front of 150 seventh graders, I went to grad school to find out why. I spent two years studying persuasion and speaking. Why do some people believe this speaker, but not another? When does persuasion flip into manipulation? Why do some movements work, and others die?

The answer can be boiled down to a real, human, *emotive* connection. (Curiously, persuading with only emotion can be dangerous. But without it, persuasion is almost pointless.) And the near-perfect container for that real, human, and emotive connection is a story.

THE BRAIN SCIENCE

As Brené Brown once said, inside the brain "we are wired for story," tapping into not just the emotive and more primitive parts of the brain, but also the most cognitively developed parts. I'm not a neuroscientist, but brain science is compelling. Take a look at some of these insights from Will Storr's *The Science of Storytelling* about the core happenings in the brain when we tell a story:

- We ignite "mirror neurons" when we see and experience another person's story, making it feel almost like we ourselves are living the story. (Wow!) In other words, a person sitting in the audience, watching our story, is also experiencing it *with* us, almost like they were there when it happened.

- The *insula* is a part of the brain located in the limbic (or emotive) system. It seeks out relatable experiences, looking for similarity and universality. What a welcome relief from our Twitter reality! Imagine your audience is sitting there, and their core intention is to find connections between your story and their life. It's as if, while they sit and take in your story, life experiences, and emotions, they're sorting through a catalog of their own life experiences to find the connection between you and them. What a powerful human instinct that happens naturally, all thanks to story!

- Stories tap into the newest, most complex part of the brain, which thrives on novelty, challenge, and our highest level of thinking. So as your audience is listening, each audience member's brain is lighting up, forming new connections, and being challenged to think deeply about life and their existence in it. It's why storytelling often inspires new perspectives, new thinking, new ideas, and new connections.

The brain science behind storytelling is persuasive—and exciting! It's incredible to know about whatever is going on up there without our awareness and knowledge while we speak our stories. I've personally seen the ways stories transform the audience in the most tangible of ways. Let me break down a bit more why stories are so powerful.

#1: STORIES ENGAGE

Have you ever had that experience where you're sitting in an audience and someone is talking about something, and they remind you of the teacher from the *Peanuts* cartoon? ("*Wah, wah, wah, wah, wah, wah, wah.*") And then they start to tell a story—and it snaps you back into attention.

It turns out that there's a reason for that as well. Our brains are especially interested in the emotion and specificity of a story. It breaks through the noise of information that dulls the senses.

One of the filters in our brain that helps us sort out the thousands (even millions?!) of pieces of data and input we take in each day is the thalamus. This filter only allows data we deem important through to us. Tapping into the specificity of a story triggers its emotional reality, which helps it slip through that filter and make it more memorable.

Let's think about the teenagers I was speaking to earlier in this book. I delivered hundreds of talks in those years, and I witnessed and coached hundreds more talks. And it was clear: The story held them captive. An audience had very limited interest in our *wah wah wah*. And who can blame them, really?

I remember standing in the back of the gym we used to present in, watching some of my speakers trying to engage a room full of teenagers. From the back, you could just see their heads bouncing around, chatting to the kid next to them, fidgeting, messing around. They were NOT engaged. But the moment the speaker shifted into a story—BOOM! We had their precious attention and focus.

Let me make it clear: Nobody appreciates the *wah wah wah*. And we're not just talking about teenagers! We as adults have just gotten used to it. We tolerate it. We've decided that being bored by the *wah wah wah* is the cost of doing business. We haven't invested the time and energy into setting higher expectations than what's expected.

So storytelling isn't useful only for finicky audiences like teenagers. They just happen to be the ones who are honest enough to let us know when they're bored. (Although I also spent a lot of time speaking to teachers—and they were pretty brutally honest, too.)

Stories belong in the business sector as much as they belong on the TEDx stage. They engage and lead people around ideas that are essential. Your next boring monthly meeting? Start with a story, and see how people engage more with your agenda. The big pitch you have coming up? Instead of trying to convince us that it's an awesome idea, speak to the heart through a story— and watch how people lean in instead of lean away. Your push to get more visible on social media not amounting to much? Share a story, and notice how people will move much more quickly from stranger to connection.

PRO TIP

When you are speaking, and you feel that sense of disengagement or antsiness from your audience, share a story. It will magically pull them in again!

#2: STORIES BREAK THROUGH BARRIERS

One of the beautiful and magical things about stories is that *they exist outside of category.* They exist outside of definition. They are one of the only things that can get past the walls that divide us and sneak past people's defenses.

Defensiveness is a challenge we have to overcome if we want to lead and create change in any way. As leaders, the whole goal is for us to step out front and actually say something. This means that what we have to say might be controversial or challenge a way of thinking—and so we need stories to break through defensiveness.

When I talk to people about speaking, sometimes my audience is full of people who resent my presence from the *very* first moment. One look, and I can tell they're sending me a major side-eye, saying, "You cannot make me stand up and speak anything today, lady!" from across the room.

These people are pretty sure they have me figured out: *She's a professional speaker. An extrovert. She LOVES this and is good at it and never gets nervous.* And they—as people who hate this, who don't want to do it, who resent even being asked to consider speaking—have their metaphorical (and sometimes literal) arms folded against me.

So I have to humanize myself and keep their defenses down. And I do it through story: Stories of me being nervous. Stories of me failing. Stories of the imperfect, stumbling, real me. (These are not hard to come by, by the way.)

Before someone has a chance to say, "Oh! This is about *this* topic, and I already know I feel *this way* about it" (aka "I'm not really listening to you"), a story sneaks in—and it gets them to empathize and feel *before* their brain categorizes your idea in the old way.

Stories help us see beyond how we've defined one another and the categories that exist in this world. If you want to change someone's mind about something, you need story.

#3: STORIES CREATE RESONANCE AND EMPATHY

As I was standing in front of those 150 seventh graders, I think it was pretty clear that I was not "one of them." I was clearly in my twenties, and I was not currently dealing with the particular challenges of living their particular lives. And yet, for my stories to impact and persuade, I needed the kids to know that I *got* them.

I had to find and tell stories that could elicit the "yes, me too" kind of response. The powerful "yes, me too" that can happen when someone tells a story is the foundation of an audience's trust—and their willingness to listen to you.

Did it require me, as the speaker, to seek to truly understand what their lives were like? Yes. Did it require me to create the story in such a way so that they knew this? Yes. And most importantly, it required me to really care.

You can't fake caring through your stories—and that caring earned me a level of interest and curiosity to start with. You earn an audience's time and attention by letting them know you "get it." And that feeling of being understood and seen makes your audience feel that they are not alone. That beautiful moment of shared humanity and connection is persuasion at work: real, emotive, and courageous.

Also, as the speaker, it's especially important to note that your story doesn't have to be the SAME as your audience's. You don't have to have lived the same life—even remotely so. You do, however, need to find a way to create resonance. (I'll show you how later in this book.)

Stories have a particular power for us to experience a moment in someone else's life without actually having to live it. This is true from both the audience's perspective and the speaker's. Stories allow us to connect with and feel experiences that are not our own.

#4: STORIES HELP THE ABSTRACT MAKE SENSE

Before I shared the story about John, courage was this abstract idea that the seventh graders couldn't quite wrap their heads around. We know what courage is, mostly. But what does it look like? What does it feel like? How does it taste, feel, or behave? As these teenagers saw John—even in their own heads, as they listened to me tell that story—the concept of courage became something tangible, real, meaningful.

Stories bypass the brain and go straight into the heart. They give an idea legs, words, actions, and feelings. They make the idea stand up and walk around on this earth, and they help us face the consequences of that idea in action. Stories help us touch it, taste it, and believe in it, in 3D.

chapter 4
What Stories Are Not

Sometimes reality is too complex.
Stories give it form.
— JEAN-LUC GODARD

Let me be clear about what stories are not.

Stories are not rants. They are not summaries of something that happened. They are not reports. They are not generic. And they are not without a point.

We're not talking about entertainment storytelling. We are sharing a very purposeful story that's going to **do something specific**. Stories are persuasive—and we're going to intentionally leverage that story to help bring your idea or your business or your message to life and connect with your audience in a more compelling way.

chapter 5

So . . . What Is a Story?

An often-repeated definition of *story* is "anything with a beginning, a middle, and an end." I like this definition, but it's important to note that stories don't have to be chronological. So let's release our definition from that expectation.

How about "a recounting of a past event or a string of events"? In other words, this happened, then this happened, and then this happened. Yes, at its core, this feels on point. But we can probably agree that's pretty simplistic and missing a lot.

This is the definition of *story* that we're going to use for this book: ***"A moment that is brought to life and whose meaning is illuminated by the words and delivery of a speaker."***

Let's break that down:

- **"A moment":** This refers to one specific moment in time.

- **"Brought to life":** In other words, we (as audience

members) experience the story in some way with you, the speaker.

- **"Whose meaning is illuminated":** Your job isn't just to bring a moment to life. It's also to create meaning from that moment for whoever is listening (aka your "audience") to help them see this moment through a particular lens and shape their understanding. More on this later; for now, know that creating meaning is a speaker's privilege and responsibility.

- **"By the words and delivery of a speaker":** The mode of communication we're using to bring this to life is your words, your delivery, and YOU! (This is the key!)

Remember, this is a particular KIND of story: the kind we tap into when we want to not just engage and entertain, but also persuade.

chapter 6
Leadership Stories

So what exactly is a leadership story? They are these three things:

#1: LEADERSHIP STORIES ARE PERSUASIVE

Stories can sneak in and convince people of things when they least expect it.

When I studied persuasion in grad school, stories were a tool I landed on because I had watched it work wonders with one of the toughest audiences out there: teenagers. I wondered, *Does it work across other audiences? Would adults face the same response to stories? What about a strictly business audience? Or a group of distracted adults?* (You could argue that they're closed-minded, logical thinkers—and worse than teenagers.)

The short answer is, yes. Great marketers and salespeople know this already, too, and they use stories wisely. Did you know that when you attach a story to your product, that story can increase the value of that product by *2706 percent*? (What?! I honestly can't believe that is even a percent.)

In other words, stories increase the value of something by *a lot.*

#2: LEADERSHIP STORIES ARE PERSONAL

Influence is created by how others feel about you and your goals.

—— ANNETTE SIMMONS

Simply put: If you want to tell a good story, it needs to be personal and emotive.

So let's not kid ourselves and think that if you're speaking in the business context, it means your "storytelling" can remain intellectually focused and emotionally distant. Because if your stories are emotionally distant, they simply won't work.

An effective story is personal because it is about what happens to you, what you observe, or what you think. It's about your perspective. If you are speaking a story, your job is to share a personal perspective. That's what makes it a leadership story, and so those stories should be personal.

That is the challenge in front of us. How do we personalize a story? Even if you're not telling your own story, or even if you are representing the story of a business, **you have to find a way to make the story personal.** Otherwise, it won't work.

#3: LEADERSHIP STORIES MAKE A POINT

Years ago, I was coaching Ben, a speaker who had some incredible stories to share. He had the kinds of stories that most of us think we have to have to be considered worth listening to. He had stories of adventure, daring, and risk-taking that were powerful and engaging, including (actually) getting chased by a brown bear and surviving. He didn't have to find the drama in the story—it was simply there in the retelling, based purely on the plot points! He leads a life most of us don't imagine for ourselves, which makes his storytelling automatically compelling.

But as his coach, I saw a huge opportunity he was missing. He would tell this brilliant story, and then . . . nothing. He would just move on to the next story, not bothering to make the point clear to that particular audience—or make any point at all. He had a point, of course; he just didn't articulate it. I'd say to him, "Ben, you're leaving too much to chance. You have no idea what lesson they're taking from your story!"

"That's the way I like it," he would say.

Now, ultimately, it was up to Ben, since he was the one speaking. He liked telling his stories and leaving them at the feet of the audience, inviting them to pick up whatever idea they felt or connected to on their own. But I have a different approach.

One of my favorite books on storytelling is *Long Story Short* by Margot Leitman. It's full of great quotes and advice on storytelling. It is thought-provoking and funny. Margot is also an award-winning Moth storyteller, and she founded the storytelling program at the Upright Citizens Brigade. She knows what she's doing.

But Margot and I differ in our thinking in one major way, much like how Ben and I differ. Margot believes that it isn't a storyteller's job to offer the moral of a story. She believes that we should lay the story down for the audience and let them take from it what they will.

Truth be told, I think there's something really artistic and beautiful about that; and in some contexts, I think that's exactly the right approach (like in a Moth StorySLAM, for example). But for us as leaders and people who are intentionally doing something with our stories, we have to take it a step further. *It's our job to create that meaning, pull out the significance of a story, and offer it up to the audience with new meaning and a new perspective.*

The truth is, stories are doing something, regardless of whether we know it. I don't want us to hit our audiences over the head with the purpose and point of our stories and talks as if they don't have the capability of doing it themselves. But it's a missed opportunity if we don't pull out the meaning, offer up our insights, and take the opportunity to help shape that new perspective. That is our privilege as speakers. You get to help shape the meaning and significance of the story—and, therefore, shape the future.

So leadership stories are *persuasive*, they're *personal*, and they have a *point*. (I love alliteration!)

chapter 7
Yes, You Have a Story to Speak

If you were sitting in the fundraising event I spoke about during the introduction, it would be easy to write off that powerful story moment as only something that the speaker could do. Clearly, he had some experience and was quite skilled. He knew what he was doing!

And that's exactly what most people think:

- "Well, THEY can do that because THEY are a speaker. I'm just a facilitator. I speak every once in a while (or when I have to)."

- "THEY can do that because THEY have a natural gift and capability. I'm not good at speaking. I'm an introvert / not a performer / not _____."

- "THEY can do that because THEY have led an interesting life! My life has been boring."

In other words, most people (including most of the people I work with) believe that those moments—and the capability to move your audience with a story—are *only* for those rare, special, elite-level "speakers," not for the average person who's just trying to figure out how to get through the day.

Will you believe me when I tell you that's simply not true? It's not.

You do have stories to share (even if you think your life is boring). Your voice matters. You don't need any special qualifications to share a needed story. In fact, the people you are trying to influence are *hungry* for you to share your stories. Sure, there are skills and approaches you can learn that will help. (You've got this book, so you've got a fantastic start!) And yes, some people have a natural inclination toward speaking.

But the skill? The captivating story? And the capability to create a moment with your audience, whoever they may be and no matter how big or small that group is? ***It can be learned.*** You can become a powerful storyteller.

Let me tell you about Dave.

Dave was one of the very first speakers I coached, way back when I was in my mid-twenties. We both worked at the nonprofit organization where we got to speak to teenagers in schools about big ideas like kindness, courage, and respect. It was a DREAM job for me. And because I came into the job with some experience already as a coach and speaker, I got tapped early on to not just speak, but also coach the other speakers in the organization.

Dave was maybe the best youth worker I've ever had the

privilege of working alongside. He is incredibly compassionate, generous, intuitive, and loving. He was a gifted teacher who had wanted a break from the classroom and was recruited into this "motivational speaker" role. It didn't come naturally to him. He loved long-term relationships with his students; he wanted to know their stories, learn about their families, and walk with them in their struggles and development.

The events we delivered were daylong experiences, so we didn't have the opportunity to spend a lot of time with the kids we were speaking with because we were only there for a few hours (and then never saw them again). To make our experiences work, we had to know how to show up and build rapport and resonance quickly. We didn't have time to build a deep relationship, so stories were the most effective and powerful tool we had—if we could tell them well.

All of this set Dave up to be an incredible classroom teacher, but not necessarily a dynamic and effective motivational youth speaker. He wasn't naturally funny, and he didn't understand comedic timing or stage dynamics well. He had powerful stories, but he didn't know how to tell them in a way that quickly engaged a large audience or kept them interested in topics that cause most teenagers to roll their eyes.

Dave and I traveled and spoke a lot together. Typically, I would give one talk, and he would give the other. Afterward, we would give each other feedback.

Let me say this: It takes courage to show up and do something you don't feel especially confident about in front of 150-plus teenagers who let you know when you're not really making the cut. And yet, there Dave was, showing up every day in front of harsh critics who didn't know him at all, trying to win them over and keep them engaged when they had no reason to care. (*sigh* There's nothing like speaking to teenagers to quickly teach you the ropes.)

You have a rough showing one day—stumbling and tripping over the stories, or not landing the point very well—and you still have to get up and do the same thing the next day. Work like this is like getting a masterclass in storytelling and speaking because every day you get to refine, and learn, and try again . . . if you can manage to refine, and learn, and try again. If you are open to learning and working hard, if you pay attention and adjust, you can get better fast.

And that's exactly what Dave did. He and I would bring our heads together after each event and talk about tweaks he (and I) could make and ideas for how to make the story and talk flow better. He experimented, and he consistently asked me for advice and ideas. I'd see him pacing the hallway before each talk, going over the changes.

Dave knew the power and potential of this art form, even if he didn't feel confident about it yet. He WANTED to be excellent at it.

On day one of our work together, I had pegged Dave as an awesome youth worker, but not a speaker. However, I will never forget the moment when I finally thought, *Wow. Dave IS a speaker.*

I was standing in the back of the room, and Dave launched into a powerful story about a student from one of his classes who had been struggling with self-respect. He dropped into his body, and into the present moment. He gave the big moment space to breathe so that everyone in the room could be drawn into it as well. He was authentic, comfortable, and present. It was POWERFUL. I almost burst into tears!

Dave showed up bravely every day and asked for my feedback nearly as often. He took that feedback to heart, working on the little and big things. And he got better at speaking.

If you have the heart for your message, and the willingness to take risks to try and improve, *you will get there*. (And it might not take the blood, sweat, and tears Dave had to shed to get there!)

Know this: There are #NoSpecialUnicorns in speaking and storytelling. You, as you are right now, are enough to show up and speak your story; and you can cultivate the tools to do it well.

Now that we understand the core foundations of story and why they're so critical for our leadership and impact, we need to do a few things:

- Become a version of you who tells stories (part 2)

- Find the stories to tell that will move your audience (part 3)

- Craft a story (part 4)

- Learn from other speakers to help you find your approach (part 5)

- Tell your stories well (part 6)

Which is exactly what we'll do in this book.

So, are you ready?

part 2

Become Someone Who
Tells Stories

chapter 8

Moving from Expert to Thought Leader

You may be coming to this book already confident in what you know. That's an important place to start! You have experience, knowledge, and topical expertise. All of these things are truly needed if you're going to stand up and speak your story.

But that can't be where it ends. Your job as a leader is to share not only what you know, but also *who you are*. And if that feels scary right now, that's okay. Stories push us to move beyond the head, step into risk, and speak from the heart in truly transformative ways.

The process of speaking your story is the process of moving from expert to thought leader. An **expert** knows things and shares what they know in the form of information. Dr. Fauci is a great example. So is a meteorologist, and sometimes a history book or a museum guide. Even Google and so many of the new artificial intelligence functions act as experts for us.

And that's great. We need experts! And we can't ultimately become a speaker without first owning our expert status. (Yes, you know enough. Yes, your experiences are enough. Yes, your knowledge is worthy!) But we can't stay in the land of the expert. We have to make the shift into thought leadership.

A **thought leader** knows things and shares what they know, but they also share who they are. This means they share stories. They share *how* they came to know what they know. Their stories and ideas are grounded in that knowledge and experience—and, more importantly, they're rooted in a vision and story for something different.

Experts share information. Thought leaders create meaning.

Ultimately, speakers are people who are shaping perspective and leading with that perspective. ("Thought leader" is one of the terms we use to express that idea.) So your job—if you want to harness the power of story—is to embrace the role of thought leadership.

Yes, I know, I know. You may be cringing at the thought leadership concept. (Too many bad TEDx Talks will do that to you.) But if you have an idea you want to share with the world (and you do), if you have a concept you want people to follow (and you do), if you have a point you want to make or something you want to convince people of (and you do!), then you need to embrace the idea of thought leadership. ***And thought leadership works better with stories!***

Let me tell you about another of my speakers, Jess.

Along with being a speaker, Jess is an Enneagram coach and

leadership consultant who helps teams and leaders move through conflict and create more productive and peaceful working environments. She knows all the things she needs to know to do her work. She has all the accolades, coaching certifications, and a master's degree to boot. She is an educator and is *educated*! She is eminently capable and skilled, and she has so much expertise and information to offer.

But telling stories? As Jess embraced the potential of her role as a speaker, she knew that storytelling would be important. Knowing it and doing it are two very different things, though. When you've been an educator and information-teacher for decades like she had been, it's hard to trust that storytelling can be not only an important companion to that information, but also the linchpin to its success.

When Jess came to me, her talks were good. She has such natural capabilities and is a gifted communicator. But the stories were generic, hidden underneath the weight of information and tools Jess trusted and was leaning on. She wasn't taking advantage of the persuasive power of stories—and it was keeping her stuck in the sea of experts, clambering for attention and recognition.

Jess told me, "I LOVE speaking. I'm desperate to do it more. It fills me up. But there's something missing from it. I know stories are important. But I'm not sure *how* to tell them well—and in a way that engages my audience."

So together, we created a more story-driven message she could share as a keynote speaker (or what I call a signature talk). One that felt more personal, more vulnerable, more real—and, ultimately, more impactful. She started to shift from purely an expert to a more story-driven, perspective-shaping thought leader.

Tens of thousands of dollars in speaking revenue and a TEDx Talk later, Jess may not necessarily be comfortable with the title of thought leader, but she is one. She is building stronger connections with her audience and becoming an authority and a go-to in her industry. And it's NOT because she is giving them more information. It's because she is showing up with a story-driven message.

That's the thing: People can get your expertise online for free right now. Without paying you a cent, they can find all the information they need without you.

It's the story that helps them decide whether they want to get their information from YOU. The story helps your audience decide if you "get" them. The story helps people know the context of the expertise and why it matters. The story helps you stand out.

(PS: Jess has taken that same story-driven approach to her social media. Just the other day, she said to me, "It works, Sally! Stories really do work.")

chapter 9

How Do You "Become" Someone Who Tells Stories?

Great stories happen to those who can tell them.
— Ira Glass

One time, I was leading a multiday workshop with one of my corporate clients, helping them learn this persuasive story framework. It was day two, and the participants had been practicing what I call a "two-minute talk" to share with the group. This was NOT a group of speakers. Rather, this was a group of middle managers who had been asked to level up their speaking and communication skills—and most of them did not have speaking on their bucket list!

But by this point in this particular workshop, I've generally lowered the bar for folks and let them know that any action and risk they take is appreciated . . . and that they're probably better at this than they think.

There was a buzz in the air when I walked in that day. People were feeling nervous, unsure. A few of them seemed excited. I chatted with a handful of people who were asking for my advice on their short talks and joking around.

And then I saw Jeanne. She was sitting at her table, arms crossed. And she looked . . . well, ANGRY.

I took a deep breath and walked over to Jeanne to see what was up. I've learned not to assume anything about people's body language and reactions because, more often than not, people are not thinking about me or my experiences nearly as much as I think they are. She could have been tired. She could have been worried about something at home. She could have been confused and in need of some clarity.

But nope. She was ANGRY. At ME.

"Hey, Jeanne," I said. "How's it going?"

"Not good," she answered.

"Okay. What's up? Anything I can help with?"

"Well." She paused, then went on a short, passionate tirade: "I hate this. I hate that you're making me do this. And frankly, I hate *you* for making me do it. I do not want to be here. I just want to leave."

(This is not the first time I've heard "I hate you" from one of my speakers. I don't take it personally. In fact, I find it kind of endearing, because I know they're facing big fears and I see it as a sign of courage to even voice those fears.)

I could see the fear reverberating off Jeanne. She could hardly even look at me.

I said, "Jeanne, I hear you. I know this isn't your thing, and that's okay."

She shot back, "You just LOOOOVE speaking. You're so happy ... and ... and ... EXTROVERTED! It doesn't mean the rest of us do!"

(She was right. I do love speaking. And yes, it's probably kind of annoying. So I duly noted that she needed to hear more about how it's hard for me sometimes.)

I hung in there before replying, "Yeah, that's fair. I know it can be kind of annoying if I'm enjoying this when it's not fun for you. But I want you to know that some of the best speakers I know are introverts—and there are a million ways you can do this. You don't have to do it like how I do it. Can you tell me a bit more about what you're nervous about? Because I guarantee you that everybody in here is also feeling the nerves—just like I do when I speak."

She turned to me, looked me straight in the eye, and said, "I am not a speaker, and I don't want to be a speaker."

"Jeanne, I promise I'm not here to make you a 'speaker.' But you are *speaking*. Is there another way of thinking about this that may help?"

She looked at me blankly.

I tried again. "Like, when you're with your team and leading a meeting. You're speaking then. What do you call that?"

Jeanne paused for a moment, then said, "Teaching. I'm a teacher in those moments."

(Bingo! I could work with that.)

"Okay! I love that! You're a teacher. What if you thought of this two-minute talk today as a teaching moment? It's just you being a teacher. No judgment. No expectations for wow or polish or performance. It's just you, teaching."

She thought about it a moment. "Okay. That feels a little better. I'll *maybe* do it. Maybe."

I took that as a major win and said, "Great. No pressure. If you decide to do it, then doing it is the goal, okay? You, as teacher."

I sensed I had gotten Jeanne as far as I was going to take her, so I left her to check in on the other participants.

When it came time to have people share their two-minute talks, one of the last people to get up was Jeanne. And let me tell you: It was awesome. Powerful, intentional, story-driven, and perspective-shaping. She was grounded, thoughtful, and so courageous. Her colleagues cheered, and I could not help but give her the BIGGEST HUG. (She reluctantly let me.) And I could tell she was so stinking proud of herself, as she should have been.

She didn't call herself a "speaker," but she indeed was a speaker. More importantly, in her speaking, she became a thought leader. She came up to me afterward and said, "I really thought I was going to hate that. But thank you."

We become by doing. And the only way there is through! Whatever you call it as you do it, doing it is how we become.

We have a lot of terms in this "speaking" world: speaker, facilitator, teacher, workshop leader, etc. To me, if you're speaking (whatever the context may be), you're a speaker. And if you're speaking with a story-driven message and with the aim to change perspective? You're a thought leader.

One of my other speakers, Tanya, had had speaking on her bucket list for years. As an entrepreneur, she hired me with the dream of getting on bigger stages and spent a full year with me, learning the nuances of creating, delivering, and scaling her story-based signature message.

Even with speaking on the big stages on her vision board, and even after investing her time and finances to hire me as her coach, Tanya would still pause whenever I'd encourage her to call herself a speaker. She'd say, "I'm not a speaker. I'm a facilitator."

"What's the difference?" I'd ask.

She'd answer, "I feel really comfortable in the workshops I do 'cause I can lean on what I know and interact with the audience. Then I'm not being a 'speaker.' I totally trust myself in those moments. It feels like I can just be me, without performing."

"How is speaking onstage different?" I asked her once. "I mean, I don't want a keynote speaker who doesn't interact with the audience any more than I want a workshop facilitator who doesn't know how to inspire and share a powerful message. We want both in both circumstances—just perhaps at different levels, based on the context."

Then I pulled out a piece of paper and drew one of my all-time favorite teaching tools: the Venn diagram. This one was for workshops and keynotes, and the two circles overlapped—a lot.

Both require story and inspiration. Both require some

educational, tactical teaching (i.e., the message and idea you're sharing). But how you do that can lean more toward a workshop style (even in a keynote setting) or more toward a keynote style (even in a workshop setting). Each context will call for something a little different.

WORKSHOP   KEYNOTE

more interaction   interaction

stories

more time   strategy   less time

more implementation   more ideas

education inspiration

The reality is, no matter what title you have or give yourself, truly becoming and embracing the title of speaker is an INTERNAL SHIFT. It turns out that the tactics and skills of speaking aren't all that different in these contexts, even if you're on a stage, under bright lights, and suddenly feeling like a total impostor.

The internal shift is about believing that you belong in that moment, that you have something to say, and that your voice and story matter. It's about doing the personal, internal work so that you know on a deep level that it's okay to take up this space, that it's okay to be *seen*, that it's okay to be *heard*.

There will be days when you'll question this truth. You'll wonder if this level of power and influence is truly within your capability. (Hint: It is.) You'll forget that it has nothing to do with how perfectly you show up, but simply in that you do show up. You'll doubt that you are as worthy, or as skilled, or as awesome as what you think is required. (And guess what? You are!) You won't believe it, but you have to take action anyway.

There are days when I question all of this, too. So keep in mind that you'll have to teach yourself the profound and simple process of finding self-trust again and again. Because once you do, you can move your audience with your story.

chapter 10
Finding Self-Trust

I am not fearless (even if it looks like I am when I'm speaking), and I have felt my share of impostor syndrome over the years. There have been some big moments in my journey when I've had to challenge myself to think of myself differently.

For example, I believed I was a speaker. But only on stages—and NOT on camera.

Even as someone who had been on some very big stages, I felt this pull to share my expertise more regularly. I wanted to be seen as an authority in my industry, to establish my own point of view and approach. I wanted to create my OWN space, rather than be invited into others' spaces.

In 2014, I considered two options: starting a video show or starting a podcast. So I started a podcast! Why? 'Cause the idea of showing my face was a nonstarter. It would make me think, *Nope. No way. Not gonna do it.*

Speaking onstage was showing my face in a way that didn't

freak me out. That felt like a safe space. I could get vulnerable onstage. But on camera?? That felt unknown and especially vulnerable. The camera work I had done up to that point made me feel like a beginner, like I suddenly didn't know what I was doing. I felt self-conscious and unsure. NO THANKS. So, a podcast it was!

Fast-forward about five years: I was watching my competitors and other entrepreneurs shifting more toward videos, and I had this sinking feeling: *I'm gonna have to tackle video.*

I wanted the authority that comes with it; I even dreamed about really rocking it on video. But I didn't want the discomfort of GETTING THERE. And I know enough to know you can't shortcut that process. (Boo.)

What it took was **the courage to show up anyway.**

And now? Well, I actually *like* video! (I didn't see that coming, but here I am, saying so now.) I had to have the courage and consistency to simply give it a go. And eventually, I started to believe it. I've taken the same path that I see all of my speakers take on their own journey to becoming a speaker and storyteller (and the same one I took years ago to become a speaker as well). With video, I went from a dream to a challenge, to the hard and sometimes humbling work of giving it a go, to finding my feet again and again . . . and to finally getting to a place of self-trust and confidence with it.

It was the same thing for Tanya. She went from the dream of wanting to be a speaker, to finally trusting herself enough a year and a half later to use the word *speaker* to describe herself. This was long after she had been speaking, but she had finally made the internal shift to embrace it.

Let me be clear: Once you're at a place of self-trust and confidence, you're not suddenly PERFECT or always AWESOME or even always ENJOYING IT. There will be days when you'll go back to the "humbling" parts to learn something new and find your confidence again. But once you've done it, you know you can do it.

But you have to do it first. The belief comes afterward.

DOING IT ANYWAY (AKA COURAGE)

Way back in the days of speaking to teenagers, my colleagues and I used to do this skit. We would pretend to be awkward teenagers, waiting in front of the school for one of our parents to pick us up; and we'd see someone really cool come by and want desperately to look cool ourselves (without much luck). All the audience of kids would hear was the voice-over of what was going on in our heads, and it would go something like this:

- "Oh, here they come. Look cool! Look cool!"

- (*with our hands in our pockets*) "Don't put your hands in your pockets. That's dumb!"

- (*putting our hands behind our heads, then sniffing our armpits*) "Ewww!"

- (*putting our hands on our hips*) "What are you? A superhero?!"

It would make the kids laugh, because it was so . . . well, accurate. (Ugh, middle school!)

Our self-consciousness during that time of life, as we're putting ourselves out there and risking rejection in such a potent way, is painful. And it reminds me so much of what it's like when we're about to speak.

In those moments, we are super aware of our bodies and suddenly forget how they work. We wonder if we know what we're talking about. We hate the sound of our voice and sweat more than we need to. (No wonder people avoid speaking, even when they have it on their bucket list!)

That self-consciousness, if we let it, can hold us back from our biggest dreams and most important purpose. It's a particular form of impostor syndrome, and no one's immune to it.

But here's the deal: In the same way I told those seventh graders to be themselves and let go of the judgment of others, I tell my speakers *every day* to be themselves and let go of the judgment of others.

Maybe you post your story on social media, and it resonates with your followers. Maybe you say yes to that LinkedIn Live request and figure out the tech well enough. Maybe you invite someone else to go live with you, and people respond to it. Maybe you go on a podcast, and it turns out you have plenty to talk about. Maybe you do a virtual summit and find new community members that way. Or, maybe you get invited to speak at an event and are seen as an authority.

Eventually, you can look back and say, "Look at that. I did it!" And little by little, you can prove to yourself that *you belong onstage.* Even if, right now, you feel like an awkward teenager.

But it requires you to SHOW UP first—and to do it consistently! Even when you're uncomfortable. Even when you're afraid. Even when you're not sure you have what it takes.

PRO TIP

It's not about showing up at all costs and sharing it all. Taking care of yourself is a must. Your level of "showing up" and sharing who you are is determined by the level of trust you have with your audience, whoever that may be. But if we let our fears dictate what we do, we'll never put ourselves in a situation of rejection—which means we'll never get better. Rejection and fear are simply a part of speaking our stories.

Your job is to move through the fear. We do this all the time when we're taking business risks, and it's no different when we face the challenge and opportunity of getting on stage. But it's not easy—and it can be a powerful barrier if we let it.

I like to think of it as the "Four Horsemen of the Avoidance" (aka the fear of speaking), because they can really haunt us:

1. **Perfection:** You want to wait until things are "perfect" (as if perfection exists), or you're forever feeling like it's "not enough." (I promise that your audience doesn't WANT you to focus on showing up perfectly!)

2. **Nerves:** You feel intimidated and nervous, and you think, *What will they think of me?!* (But if you can

turn that fear into excitement, you can leverage all that powerful energy!)

3. **Ego and Judgment:** You think you want to do this . . . but is that even okay? It's drawing lots of new eyes onto you, which is great—and scary. (But you, my friend, get to take up space and share your voice despite the naysayers!)

4. **Impostor Syndrome:** You think, *Who even AM I to think I can do this?!* (Well, YOU are a big deal. And you don't need a book, a zillion followers, or a fancy blazer to make a big impact!)

Please know this: Your discomfort, and even your fear, is a sign that you're growing and creating new realities. It may mean you're learning. It may mean you're even "failing" (even though I don't use that word in this realm!) because it actually means you're growing.

Every step, every effort, every try or trip, every moment of brilliance or humiliation is the process of moving *through* discomfort—and realizing that you're okay. (Even if it didn't FEEL okay.) Every time you step out front and SURVIVE, you prove to your body, your self-doubting mind, and your protective brain that you didn't—and won't—die. (Seriously. That's what we're teaching our brains.)

And the thing is, it's scary to step out front and show up fully. Your body and brain might really show up in discomfort while you do this. All that sweating and shaking and heart palpitating? It's your body trying to protect you. But the more you do it, the more you prove that you CAN do it (even if you're not doing it as well as you want to yet) and the faster you'll convince yourself that YOU'VE GOT THIS.

This is how you build toward self-trust—and how you become someone who speaks stories. (And once you've got self-trust? Well, this "wowing onstage" thing becomes much easier!)

The only way is through. And the more you show up (no matter what happens in that moment), the closer you move toward self-trust.

Sparks—Part 2: Become Someone Who Tells Stories
SUMMARY

Part 2 is all about becoming someone who owns their identity as a speaker and storyteller. We are shifting from the safe land of the "expert" to the more daring, powerful, and courageous identity of speaker and thought leader. Thought leaders are speakers, and this kind of speaker leverages the power of story to shift perspective and move their audience.

So, beyond the skills required for speaking, the more important shift is the process of *becoming*. This is about making the internal, personal process of finding self-belief through doing. Because it's the only way!

EXERCISES
How to #ShowUpAnyway and Cultivate Self-Trust

- **Put it in your plan.** Mark your calendar with specific times to "get visible" and share your voice and story—and stick with it. (Even if you're not feeling it in the moment, because the body will find lots of reasons not to "feel it" in the moment!) This requires discipline as well as walking directly into the discomfort.

- **Embrace the idea of "ready enough" versus feeling "ready."** You might never feel ready. There's always more you can do. But since we're not focused on showing up perfectly, the goal is to DO and LEARN.

- **Identify the fear and transform it into excitement.** Ask yourself, "Is this fear real and actually dangerous? Or is it just trying to protect me from something that is a necessary part of the process of connecting with an audience? What would happen if I decided that my fear is actually excitement?" Fear and excitement are nearly identical internal experiences; we simply perceive the feeling differently. Remember that rejection and failure are a natural (and expected) part of speaking your story. So, what if you looked at your fear differently? What if it's actually excitement in disguise?

A Mantra to Help You Consistently and Courageously Speak Your Stories

Okay, right now, roll your shoulders back. Lift your spine so you're tall and proud. Take a deep breath . . . and take up more space.

It may sound funny, but one of the things I say to my speakers again and again is to take up more space. (I say it a lot to women and bigger men, both of whom may be more likely to unconsciously try and take up less space.)

The truth is, I'm talking about how they hold their bodies physically. But it's also metaphorical. That feeling when we aren't sure whether we belong? Or when we're wondering if we really have what it takes? *It makes us small.*

Well, you have what it takes, and you deserve to take up space. Even if you have some skills to learn, you are capable. (I promise you that. I've been doing this for a long time.)

So, take a moment. Stand up. Take a deep breath. Close your eyes, roll your shoulders back, and imagine yourself on your dream stage, about to speak your story. Your heart is pounding . . . and right now, you need to remind yourself that you are worthy of this moment.

Now, repeat after me:

I am worthy.

I am worthy of taking up more space.

I am worthy of this moment.

It's okay for me to show up.

It's okay for me to be the center of attention.

It's okay for me to have something to say—and even ruffle some feathers.

I matter.

My body is powerful exactly as it is right now.

My voice, my ideas, and my message matter.

And I cannot wait to share them with my audience.

As you face your fears about speaking your story, know that you're not going to die. You're just uncomfortable. Fear is along for the ride, but she doesn't get to make the decisions—until she finally reveals herself as excitement!

TOOLS AND RESOURCES

As part of the #ShowUpAnyway Email Series, you'll get an email every morning for seven days with a prompt for how to show up and speak a story to your audience through social media. These "free stages" are a powerful platform to practice some of the skills in this book. The key is "showing up anyway."

Grab the #ShowUpAnyway Email Series here:

part 3

Finding Your Stories

chapter 11
Signature Stories

Are you thinking right now, *I don't have any stories to tell?* Don't worry. I have been there. In fact, every time I sit down to write and create a story to speak, I think the same thing: *My life is so boring! I don't live a life people would want to hear about. All I do is work, then run the kids to a zillion activities, then watch some Netflix if I have the energy, and then go to bed. And then I hit Repeat the following day. That's not really the stuff of engagement, Sally.*

Okay, you're right. That summary of my day is definitely NOT the stuff of engagement or story dreams! Telling a version like that of your day may get some appreciative nods or responses like, "Yep, I live that boring life, too!" And that's not nothing! But it's not what we're going for here.

The truth is that underneath the "boring" parts of our lives are powerful stories that can be the heart of our messages—if we take the time to see them this way.

I call any story that becomes the heart of a message a **signature story.** Sometimes these signature stories are at the heart of a **signature talk** (a repeatable, scalable, profitable message, like a keynote). Other times, they are at the heart of a live stream on social media, a moment in a panel discussion, or an introduction at an event. Any speaking moment can be grounded in a signature story.

These signature stories come in all forms and types. I'd like to introduce you to three of the most common kinds of signature stories that my speakers and I use.

#1: EVERYDAY STORIES

In 2014, I started a podcast, *This Moved Me*, about the art of public speaking and moving your audience. (At the time I'm writing this, I have done over 350 episodes, and it's become a library of content I'm incredibly proud of.) At the end of all of my interview episodes (which feature some truly incredible speakers and thought leaders from around the globe, including speakers of the ten most watched TED Talks in the world), we would spend about ten minutes talking about a This Moved Me Moment.

I would start by asking my interviewees, "What's moving you right now?" The idea was that if we want to move our audience, then we need to understand what is moving audiences—and also how *we* are moved.

Each interviewee would share with me a whole range of

moments from their life, from supporting a friend going through a difficult time, to a tender exchange in the airport, to a poem they read recently, to a hilarious video that had just gone viral. It was a full range of emotions and experiences, and it was always my favorite part of the interview. I learned so much about the speaker, and it gave me a moment to pause and ask myself the same question: "What's moving ME right now?"

And honestly, as a mom of three, I spend a lot of my day running around, feeling like a chicken with my head cut off—and it doesn't leave a lot of space for inspiration or wisdom to come to me. That's a problem! I need to be cultivating wisdom I can pass along to my audience, or I cannot be in full service to my audiences or my speakers. My ideas and perspective are gained through experience, observation, and reflection. So this question about what's moving me isn't just about filling a content gap. It's about a point of view that can be shared with an audience. It's about finding stories that can be at the heart of my messages.

But sometimes, I would come up empty-handed. What moments or stories do I have to share? I would think, *It's lucky I got here and pressed Record at all! Let alone show up with something profound to share.*

And then I remembered this moment with Scott Voss from Episode 005 of *This Moved Me:* Using Stories to Empower. Whenever I have trouble coming up with a This Moved Me Moment, I remember what Scott (a former speech coach of mine, and a genuinely awesome human) said to me: "Well, if you can't find a This Moved Me Moment, you're really not paying attention, are you?"

Yep. That's it. Life is magical—if we can take the time to see it. If I was empty-handed in that moment, it wasn't because life itself is boring. It was because I wasn't paying attention to the moments happening around me.

In the same way, I have a feeling you're missing out on a bunch of life that happens in between those obligations and the Netflix time. The trick is, **Are we SEEING the stories that surround us each and every day?**

Our job as storytellers and leaders is to help our audience SEE things differently. And so we must start by, as one of my dear friends and fellow entrepreneurs Tiffany Mattick suggests, "seeing with story eyes."

When you're working, what do you notice? Are you paying attention to the interactions? The little things that happen between coworkers? Your reaction or thoughts about a particular moment? When you're driving your kids from activity to activity, what's the conversation like? What stirs your insides or tickles your fancy? What got you teary? What pissed you off? What struck you about that Netflix show you watched? Or the book you're reading? Or the podcast you're listening to?

Essentially, part of your job as a speaker and storyteller is to pay attention to *what's moving YOU*. And if you're not being moved daily? My guess is that you're not paying attention, or not creating needed space in your life to "see with story eyes." It's easier said than done—but it's not a nice-to-do. It's a must. These moments are needed fodder and continued purpose for speaking your story. Because the only way for us to move our audience is to know what moves us as well.

#2: CUSTOMER STORIES

The easiest and most accessible stories to tell are the stories of your customers, clients, and/or employees. Basically, you're sharing their wins and struggles! They're all around you—and those stories are a fabulous way to build awareness, connection, and social proof (aka proof that what you're doing works)!

Why are these stories so much easier to share? For most people, it's easier to talk about other people than it is to talk about themselves. Customer stories are often easier to share because they feel less vulnerable. No ego, and no bragging. Rather, we're pointing people's attention to others rather than to ourselves.

PRO TIP

Customer stories cannot be the only stories you share! For me, a tried-and-true Minnesotan, this is a common struggle. Humility is a cherished Midwestern value, which is great. Humility is important. But if we only tell the stories of our customers and never share our own leadership stories and struggles, we are not stepping into thought leadership. We are simply a messenger. So even though customer stories are important, they cannot be the only stories we share.

#3: ORIGIN STORIES

When I was about nine years old, I would lie in bed at night listening to a cassette tape (yes, I'm that old) of the story of Martin Luther King Jr. There I was, a middle-class white girl, in the middle of the very white suburbs, listening to a story about a revolutionary Black man from another time who experienced things that sounded barbaric to me. I remember lying there, hearing his words and feeling *moved* by them.

How could that happen? I'd think. *Why would people treat others like that? Why??*

I didn't understand it, but I felt it. I felt the horror, the frustration, the injustice—and I knew in my core that it wasn't right. Obviously, these values were passed on to me by my parents and my community, but there was something about that moment that helped it sink in deeper.

My life is clearly different from MLK's, and of course I lead a privileged life as a white person that keeps me from truly understanding or appreciating the real pain of racial injustice. But the story—the words, the passion, the moments shared on that cassette tape—helped me *see* this different life and tap into the emotive experience required for change.

It was one of the first moments where I got to see how stories really can move the world. It's also a moment I look back to again and again as the source of my belief in the power of speaking stories in connecting people, creating powerful change, and inspiring engagement in ideas you might otherwise appreciate but not integrate.

This moment from my nine-year-old life is one of my core origin stories, the final category of signature stories we're looking at together. An origin story is exactly what it sounds like: a story about the origin, or beginning, of something.

Origin stories don't need to be dramatic or life-changing. They are simply at the root of any aha moment you've had. Every idea started somewhere. So what was that aha moment for you? The point when you realized something? That's an origin story.

Perhaps it's the story of the moment you got the idea for your business. Or the moment you discovered a new process or approach. Or the moment you took a big risk that led you to where you are now. Great stories are built on powerful aha moments. So what are yours? That's where you'll find a story that needs to be shared.

chapter 12

How Can We Cultivate These Stories in Our Life?

If you want to leverage the power of story to influence and persuade, finding stories to speak needs to become a daily habit.

We can't find the stories, no matter what kind, if we don't create these habits in our lives. Leaders who use stories consistently have a story system in place, and it's built on these three ideas.

#1: FEED Your Brain (aka Executive Mode)

My husband, Andy Zimney, speaks nationally about productivity, creativity, and how we can get unstuck in the creative process and get more done. During these talks, he speaks about the different modes of our creative genius.

The first mode is **Executive Mode**. This is when we're focused on a topic, working on something, thinking about something, and putting intentional effort into it.

When our brains are in Executive Mode, they're taking in information. We need to feed our brains with interesting information and experiences, like great shows, podcasts, travel, live music, interesting people, inspiring conferences, and thought-provoking books. There's SO MUCH to take in and feed our brains.

The truth is, as a species right now, we are spending more and more time in Executive Mode—and less and less time in the essential second mode.

#2: Create SPACE to process (Mind-Wandering Mode)

Then there's **Mind-Wandering Mode**, where we are NOT doing the above. Our mind is wandering and free: in the shower, taking a quiet walk, meditating, driving, even sleeping.

Have you ever had an aha moment? If so, when did it strike? Most likely, it struck when you were in Mind-Wandering Mode. When our brains are in this mode, they are synthesizing, processing, putting the pieces together, and making connections from all that information.

If we don't have enough "mind-wandering" in our life, we miss out on the aha moments. We need both modes to create perspective to share in our stories. But most of us need to focus on and create more space in our lives to slow down and PROCESS all the information we're taking in through Executive Mode. And none of this can really be leveraged for impact unless we're in the third mode.

#3: CAPTURE and COLLECT those aha moments

I can tell you this: It's hard to think of a story in the moment or under an urgent time constraint or deadline. Our lives are full of stories that we just aren't thinking about—or that we simply don't remember. We are struck by beautiful or funny moments that may be powerful in illuminating a moment for our audience. But if we can't remember them—or if we forget they ever happened—then we lose out on the opportunity to really impact our audience.

So we need a place to put our stories—and a way to organize them.

PRO TIP

Create one place (e.g., a document, your notes app, a voice memo) to put your ideas and stories. Then, whenever you remember a moment from your life, dump it there so it doesn't slip away. That way, when those stories come to you, you can capture them in that place—because you don't want to let those stories slip away! They are precious, and each of them might be *the* story your audience needs to hear at some point. Those stories hold the inspiration, insight, and connection we are looking for and working toward.

chapter 13
The Power of Pathos

*Aim lower underneath the rational thought to where
we can feel the same thing.*

—— ANNETTE SIMMONS

In grad school, I got to study persuasion, which meant I also had
to spend a lot of time thinking and learning about Aristotle and
his three appeals. If you're not familiar with these appeals, let
me give you a quick primer on logos, ethos, and pathos.

Logos

Logos is the logical appeal. Utilizing logos is about rational and
logical thinking. It's all about left brain activity; facts, statistics,
and objective thinking all live in the realm of logos. And a lot of
people hold tightly onto logos. We can't argue with facts (as long

as those facts are really facts—but that's a diatribe for another time). Some people believe that logos is the only place where persuasion should happen.

One of the tragedies of the progressive political approach is the belief that logic *should* be the way we persuade and are persuaded. Just stick to the facts, ma'am, and the rational mind will win out.

Case in point: John Kerry. I was in grad school when he was running for president, studying his speeches and lamenting his lack of pathos. It was all intellectual debate. No wonder he didn't win—we didn't feel connected to him! It didn't matter that he was smarter or had a more complex and thorough approach to things. He leaned on his brain—and the brain can only get us so far.

The result? John Kerry had people's respect, but not their passion or drive to advocate for and champion him. He lost the race (obviously).

The bottom line is, logos is an essential starting point, but it's not as powerful as people think it is.

Ethos

Ethos is the ethical appeal. Ethics is about who you are, what you believe, and the way you've organized your system of morality and right versus wrong. Some people use ethos as an operating mode when they're trying to persuade somebody, and it can be really effective. However, ethos is very personal and subjective. An "I believe" statement can be quickly rebutted with someone else's "Yes, but *I* believe . . ." So yes, ethos is clarifying, but it's also limited.

Pathos

Then we get to **pathos**, or the emotional appeal. Think about the root of the word *empathy*. Pathos is feeling FOR someone else. Now, the realm of pathos has been disregarded forever. Aristotle looked at these three appeals and was like, "Yes, logical appeal is the highest form. Ethics is also really important. And then pooh-pooh on the pathos. It's the lowest form of persuasion."

Okay, he didn't say "pooh-pooh." But basically he was saying that emotion is for girls and girls are dumb. Oh, Aristotle.

Now, I think we can all find examples where pathos is absolutely being used as a manipulative form of persuasion. Emotion without logic or ethos backing it up is truly dangerous and sadly rampant right now (e.g., fake news, not believing in science, conspiracy theories). Much of that can be directly related to pathos gone wild, without a logical check. Pathos without logic is called manipulation—and that is (obviously) not what I'm recommending here.

But when we are in the realm of story, we're in the realm of pathos. Without pathos, logos and ethos are less effective—and sometimes don't have a chance.

Pathos is essential if we really want to persuade people. It means speaking lower—lower than logos, like Aristotle said, but also lower as in where it exists in your body. When we are talking about feeling, we are talking about something from your gut instead of up in your head. We can only get so far when we speak from the head. So part of what I'm pushing you to do is to speak lower, to dig deeper. Like Annette Simmons said, you're going underneath rational thought to where we feel the same thing.

And it *is* harder. We've got to dig deeper to find that place where we can connect on that level. That's where the big stuff happens. That's the kind of message or story that has teeth to it, that punches you in the face (in a good way), that reaches out from the speaker to the audience. That's what changes you.

That is called connection. Pathos is how we move people.

chapter 14
To Hell with Facts

To hell with facts. We need stories.

— KEN KESEY

I realize you may be thinking, *So ... what about FACTS, SALLY?! Surely you're not saying that facts don't matter?!*

Listen, facts are important. But they're not as persuasive as we think they are. However, when coupled with stories, they can be not only powerful but also beautiful.

When you think about stats that have had an impact on you, what was probably true about that statistic was that underneath it was some emotion. If it connected with you, there was a sense of how it impacted humanity and human beings behind the stats. And essentially, that's what stories do.

Let's take this example: According to World Vision, 689 million people live in extreme poverty (i.e., on less than $1.90 a day). That number—*689 million*—is an overwhelming stat. It doesn't sound good. You know it's bad in the most generic sense. But it's hard to make that stat meaningful. How many is one million, let alone 689 million?

However, if you told me the story of Theresa, an eight-year-old who's living in poverty, that number now has a name—and maybe a face. And as I learn more about Theresa, I can start to visualize her. She's struggling with school because she comes home hungry every day and is busy taking care of her siblings. Her future opportunities are bleak if she can't go to school. But she doesn't have a lot of choices, because she's an eight-year-old girl in an impossible situation she has very little control over.

I am starting to get a glimpse of Theresa's life. I have a sense of her story, her challenges—and I'm connecting with her in an emotive way.

Now, when I hear that there are *689 million people* who are living like Theresa? That stat has significance. It has meaning. I understand what it means even more. I know what's at stake, the harm that it's causing, and why it matters. I still can't totally grasp the number 689 million, other than it's a lot. But now I know how harmful even ONE person with that story is.

Stories help enlighten stats. They make facts meaningful and personal, which then makes those facts incredibly powerful. As Luigi Pirandello once said, "A fact is like a sack—it won't stand up if it's empty. To make it stand up, first you have to put in all the reasons and feelings that caused it in the first place."

People are tired of information. Even overwhelmed by it. There's so much of it out there. Without a story, we aren't sure what that information MEANS. Stats and data alone don't do the trick. So if you're stuck in the realm of logos, it's time to come into the realm of pathos. When we combine these two appeals, they're incredibly powerful together.

So, now we know that stories are all around us if we have the eyes (and time and space) to see them. We also know that stories need to be emotively driven (and look beyond the logical appeal). And finally, we know that behind every fact is a story.

chapter 15
Excavating Our Stories

Tell the story that's been growing in your heart, the characters you can't keep out of your head, the story that speaks to you, that pops into your head during your daily commute, that wakes you up in the morning.

—— JENNIFER WEINER

The process of identifying and discovering the stories in our lives is an exploration that doesn't end with this book. Even if you're fairly sure of a story you want to speak, creating an authentic and impactful story-based message requires you to do some excavating of your lessons learned, your big aha moments, and your core content areas. Only then can you build a powerful, memorable, and compelling story.

The magic of a persuasive story is different than it was even ten years ago. It used to be okay to "sell, sell, sell" and have it be all about the business. (Some people still do this!) But with the advent of the TED Talk and the continued shift toward that approach, our job is now to "serve, serve, serve." We are not promoting our business. ***We are promoting an idea.***

We all know that stories can be a powerful marketing and promotional tool. So the magic of your story is that it reflects not just your business (though it's not about your business), but also YOU: your particular spirit, language, and approach. And your story cannot exist in a world without the context of your audience and what they really need, given the world that we live in (and the way your business attends to those needs). That beautiful middle point is where we want to aim our story: a mix of your business, you, and the world.

YOUR MOVING MESSAGE

Let's take a moment and look at how these three elements come together in a Venn diagram (because I really do love Venn diagrams!) that I call your Moving Message.

YOU

With you, we are looking for *distinctions*. So here are some questions you can ask about your distinctions to begin creating your Moving Message:

- What are your passion points?

- What pisses you off about your industry?

- Where do you, they, or we need to do better?

- What makes you different compared to your competition?

YOUR AUDIENCE

Now, let's think about your audience using these questions:

- Who is your audience? In other words, who are they?

- What does your audience believe (generally speaking, of course)?

- Where are they struggling?

- What themes have you found about their psychosocial reality?

- Who do you love working with? Why?

let's put them together:

How can you - in particular - help your audience with their particular challenges?

YOU + YOUR AUDIENCE

Now, when you think about your gifts and point of view, how can *you* serve this particular *audience*, given their particular challenges and needs?

THE WORLD

Finally, we layer on the last part of the diagram: the world and your business in it (aka your purpose). Here are some questions to consider about this aspect of your Moving Message:

- What's happening in the world right now that your business addresses?

- What is the market demanding of your business right now? (A speaker in the education field, for example, cannot serve their audience the same way now as they did before the COVID-19 pandemic.)

- How does the context of the world and the market change how you show up and serve your audience?

- How is your purpose evolving so that you can serve your audience in the context of NOW?

WHAT HAPPENS WHEN THESE THREE IDEAS COME TOGETHER?

You—authentically and specifically YOU—are serving the particular needs of your audience, in the context of the world and your business living and breathing in that world. That's your Moving Message!

Once you've gotten clearer on your Moving Message—an exercise that's worth doing at least once a year—it will clarify your purpose and help you adjust it to the world and the changing needs of your audience. And it's step one in ensuring that your story-based message is grounded not just in what you feel like speaking about, but also in what is needed from your audience and in response to the market and the world as they are.

chapter 16

Putting Your Signature Story in Your Message

Now that we've thought about how to bring more of YOU out into the world through your overall message and how to do it in a way that serves your audience and your business, we need to make sure that your story is going to point directly at what you just got clear about. In other words, we need to make sure that whatever story you choose is reflective of your Moving Message.

Here's the Message Hierarchy, a powerful framework that has helped my speakers clarify each story they tell to ensure it's hitting the mark.

To get a clearer picture of your signature story, we start with the most basic of questions: *What do you want to be known for?* Or, as I like to think of it, what's your "take" on your topic or industry? Let's use this image to help us.

message
HIERARCHY
for example!

YOUR TOPIC

YOUR 'TAKE' ON YOUR TOPIC

Your industry or topic area is the rain—and let's be real, there are a lot of people speaking in your industry, likely on the same topic. There are lots of "experts" out there! In some industries, it's absolutely pouring rain with speakers speaking about the same topic.

So how can you open your umbrella and create a dry, safe, and defined space that is just yours? A place where people can seek out shelter? This is where your Moving Message comes in— and where your differentiation can help you open that umbrella and create space in your industry that is just yours.

Let's take my own Message Hierarchy as an example. My industry or topic is speaking. (Ooooh, it's a rainy industry! Like monsoon season! So many speaker coaches are out there!) So how do I differentiate myself?

My "take" on the topic is that authentic, story-based speaking is how you move your audience. Each of those words is a differentiator for me: my dual focus on authenticity and a story-based, story-driven message—all to not just impact or impress an audience, but also *move* them. All the perfect gestures, the lack of filler words, the obsession over image, and the polishing-away-of-our-humanness bologna do not matter.

And that belief, that "take," should be seen and felt in *every* story I share. Where does that belief come from? There's a story there!

And it's likely a signature story that is essential for you to identify and speak about regularly. When I'm consistently sharing signature stories that uphold my "take," it helps me underline my point of view and establish myself as an expert and authority. It also differentiates me from my competition in a way that isn't just smarty-smart, but also meaningful, personal, and FELT.

chapter 17

Clarifying the Idea behind Your Story

Before we can create a story, we need to do one final clarification of your *idea* that will make it much easier for you to find the stories you need to tell. In the previous chapter, you asked yourself, "What do I want to be known for?" And that's a powerful place to start.

But it's likely not specific enough to find the *most* signature story for you to speak. You are here to DO something. So what do you want to DO with your story? What change do you want to create?

At first blush, this might be simple. But for a lot of people, the idea is kind of like an onion that we haven't peeled down enough yet. So to peel down into the idea, we have to think about finding what I call our **thesis statement**. In other words, what is the point of this story? What is it leading toward? And one of the best ways to do that is to keep asking yourself, "So what?"

For example, let's say you want to be known for transforming the health care system. That is your idea. But right now, it's quite broad and generic. So we ask, "So what? Why do you need to do that?"

Now, let's say this is your answer: *Because health care isn't accessible enough to people.*

Then we ask, "So what? Why is that important?"

Maybe this is your next answer: *Well, minority populations are suffering more than other people.*

And so we ask again, "So what?" Peel that onion. Keep getting more and more specific.

Maybe you give this answer next: *Urban residents don't have access to enough healthy food, and it's affecting their capability to lead full lives.*

Wow. That's really different from simply transforming health care. Now we're transforming a really specific slice of this very broad category. Now we are onto something.

And now, all of a sudden, there's a story baked into that intention. It's probably going to be much easier to find your story once you drill down far enough with the "So what?" test.

PRO TIP

Please note that this process of creating your story is an evolving one. It's iterative. So you may start with a particular thesis statement idea, then find a story that helps clarify and lead you to a slightly different thesis statement. It can go back and forth like that for a bit.

Sparks—Part 3: Finding Your Stories
SUMMARY

In part 3, we explored the process of finding stories that are aligned with you, your audience, and the context of the world that your business is attending to. These signature stories are driven by pathos (not just logic) and require us to create space to "be moved" so that we can turn around and move our audience with our stories. We want to find—and consistently collect and capture—stories that share and illuminate our differentiating point of view (aka our "take") so that our stories help us stand out from the crowd of experts that also speak in our industry.

EXERCISES
Brainstorm Your Stories

Keep in mind the following things:

- One story can have many uses.

- The story doesn't have to be about you.

- Your story doesn't have to be directly about your topic, but it should relate to the topic. In other words, it can be metaphorical.

- Look for moments of change and pivot, as well as before and after moments.

- Remember, a story can be the smallest of moments. We do need some sense of what you might call drama, but drama exists in the everyday. We just don't often see it or find meaning in it.

- Your story doesn't have to be life-altering. Your perspective and insight will bring the drama!

- Make your story about a specific moment. This is critical!

PRO TIP

If you're wrestling with deciding which story to create, just pick something. No story is going to be perfect, and most stories can be made more effective over time.

Ideas to Get You Started with Brainstorming

- What's moved you recently?

- What are some "Before and After" moments? What are those moments where something happened—and then things were different in some way?

- What's an aha moment that changed your perspective?

- When you're hanging out with friends, what's your favorite story you tell?

- What's a family story that gets told again and again when your family gets together?

- What's a moment when everything changed?

- What's a moment you don't like to share? Or that feels especially vulnerable?

- If you were to let risk be your compass, what story would you share?

- If you didn't worry about how others would react, what story would you share?

JOURNAL QUESTIONS

1. Write about a big aha moment from your life. What was it? What happened? Who was there? Describe the experience and what you learned from it.

2. Sometimes defining what you stand AGAINST is a helpful way to define your passion points and point of view. What upsets you? Where do people need to be moving toward? What are you willing to stand for? Or piss off other people about?

3. At your funeral, what do you hope to hear people say

about the impact you've had? What is the legacy you are creating?

4. Write about three influential people in your life and one specific moment with each of them. What did they teach you? What was their legacy for you? How have they impacted you?

TOOLS and RESOURCES

In part 3's "Tools and Resources" (that you can find by visiting the QR Code on the next page), you can grab this story log:

STORY	PILLAR 1	PILLAR 2	PILLAR 3
SCUBA DIVING STORY	X	X	

In this log, you can keep track of your stories (like "Scuba Diving Story," as shown in the far left column), then categorize each story as it applies to different pillars in your business. A **pillar** is a topic or idea that you often speak about. For example, if you talk a lot about authenticity, leadership, or conflict, name those as some of your pillars, listing one pillar each in columns two, three, and four.

That way, whenever you log a story, you can also determine how you may want to use it, or what idea that story can illuminate or relate to. Then, when you are looking for a story on authenticity, for example, you'll have a few stories at the ready!

You can also grab two messaging worksheets: the Moving Message Worksheet and the Message Hierarchy Worksheet. Both of these are blank versions of the models you saw in part 3.

Grab these resources here:

part 4

How to Create Your
Leadership Story

chapter 18
The Moment and the Meaning

I am a swimmer—a really good swimmer. And for whatever reason, I'm terrified of scuba diving in the ocean. But there I was, on my honeymoon (many years ago!) with my husband, and he really wanted to go scuba diving.

Maybe it was a naive sense of my duty as a new wife? Or maybe I was feeling brave and wanting to, you know, live a story-worthy life? But most likely, I was drawn in by the bane of every Enneagram Seven's existence: *But what if it's awesome?!* So I said, "Sure, okay."

Oceans are sort of like space. Like, what is down there? It's the great unknown. And I don't really have any interest in "knowing it." So, again, why was I going scuba diving?

I was nervous, but you know what? It was a great lesson in marriage! *It's really important to him,* I thought back then. *Compromise and making it work for each other and BLAH, BLAH, BLAH. And who knows? Maybe I'll think it's awesome.*

The first moment I got a sense that this scuba diving adventure was going to be a harrowing experience was on the boat ride over to our diving spot. After I had told the instructor I was an adept swimmer, and because everybody else in the group had scuba dived so many times before, the instructor decided to skip the part where he would train us in the pool. Instead, he would do a truncated training—in the ocean.

(What?!)

And there I was, as he was explaining how to BREATHE UNDERWATER on the way over in the boat.

I remember flying across the Caribbean on the catamaran, soaring across the huge waves, and the instructor's flipping through a big chart, saying, "Okay. Well, first you're going to hop into the water, and then you're going to take out your breathing apparatus, and then you're going to put it back in. And if you can pass that, then you can go on the dive. And if you can't, you can't."

And I was like, *I'm sorry. WHAT?! We have to take out the breathing thing in the water? Isn't that how you stay alive?!* ("Breathing thing" is not the technical term, but I'm pretty sure the instructor knew what I was talking about.)

At that moment, I thought, *I don't want to do this. I don't want to do this.* But, of course, nobody else is freaking out. And so, like a good Midwestern girl, I just rolled right along in the boat, internally freaking out.

Eventually, we found our spot in the Caribbean, and I looked out over the boat into a vast view of . . . water. Just . . . water. *There better be something amazing down there,* I thought, *'cause right now, I do NOT want to do this.*

Everybody else got into the water and did their pretest. They took their breathing tubes out and put them back in. No problem. Even Andy hopped into the water and passed his pretest. And so everyone was treading water about ten or fifteen yards out from the boat, waiting for me.

I was the last one to go. Andy swam up really close to the boat, and I tentatively got into the water. As I slid in, my eyes must've been huge, because Andy kept calling out to me, "Sally, it's going to be okay. You're going to be okay. You can do this."

I will never, ever, *ever* forget the moment when the instructor put the weights on my waist so that I started to sink. I was holding onto my mouthpiece like it was my only tie to life (which is exactly what it was). As I started to sink, the water rose above my mouth, then my eyes, and then my head. All I could think was, *The body cannot breathe underwater. This is wrong. Get me out of here. Get me out of here!*

It was a harrowing experience. I mean, I was nervous, but I didn't think it would be scary. But it *was* scary. I held on to the instructor's wet suit for the entire first dive. While we swam around, I kept one hand on him and the other on my breathing mouthpiece. It stayed that way until about halfway through the second dive. (Yes, I went on a second dive.)

On the second dive, I finally let the instructor swim about five yards away from me. I (sort of) remember seeing some (sort of) cool things. I vaguely remember some fish, and a sunken boat. By the end of it, I was like, *Maybe, just maybe, I would do that again in my lifetime.*

(PS: That was twenty years ago, and I've never gone scuba diving again.)

Here's what's cool about this story: When I speak, I share it to do all kinds of different things. I share it to talk about fear. I share it to talk about using our voice. I share it to talk about trying new things, what happens to our bodies when we're afraid, or how we sometimes respond in surprising ways. There are a lot of things that I can do with that story.

As you think about your story, you might use it in different ways depending on who you're talking to, where you are, and what message is most needed.

To help you decide which story to share, as well as what you want to say about that story, you want to think about two things:

1. **The Moment** (i.e., the story)

2. **The Meaning** (i.e., what you want to DO with that story, and how the story can connect to your audience)

With the scuba diving story, you have the **moment**, which is me scuba diving. And then you have the **meaning**, which is the point you want to make from that story based on the context you're in, who you're talking to, and what they need. In this case, the point may be about fear, courage, or using your voice.

PRO TIP

There's an important additional benefit to storytelling I want to point out. When I share this story of me scuba diving, you also get to know me a little bit. Through the story, you get a peek into me as a three-dimensional human being. Here's me, struggling. Here's me, freaking out. Here's a sense of my relationship with Andy. You get to know me more so that I become more of a fully dimensional human being for you, instead of an "expert" out front who is difficult to relate to. I become a person who I hope you feel more connected to now.

This distinction between the moment and the meaning is powerful and important—and it's what makes a story about you matter to your audience.

Here's another concrete example. One of my clients was preparing for a big summit on equity that she was speaking at. We had been working on stories she might tell (aka the moment) and answers she could give on this panel.

A few days before the summit, my client and I realized this event would take place two days after a big midterm election—and whatever happened during that election would change the conversation in the room. It would change how people would be feeling in the room. It would change the questions that would be asked and the concerns of the audience. And it would require me and my client to adjust what the audience really needed to hear from her (aka the meaning).

Our job as leaders and speakers is to be intentional about not just the moment, but also the meaning we're creating. The craft of a great story requires our intentionality about both aspects: how we bring the specific moment to life *and* how we're going to make that moment meaningful for that particular audience. And that can change dramatically depending on what *you need*, what *the audience needs*, and what *the moment calls for*.

So, how do you prepare for the specific context? How do you adapt your moment so that it creates the meaning your audience needs?

chapter 19

Do a SASI Analysis

Storytelling offers an opportunity to talk with your audience, not at them.

—Laura Holloway

When you're speaking, context is truly king. You can create a beautiful story. But if you aren't thinking about context, you can't create the meaning that your audience needs (or you might accidentally create the wrong or unhelpful meaning they don't really need).

Here's one of my favorite tools: a SASI[1] analysis you can do before each message or story you speak. SASI stands for:

- **Speaker:** Who you are

---

1. SASI is an adaptation of the theater term AASI (Actor, Audience, Space, and Idea), which helps theater producers and creatives think through all the elements of creating a theatrical production.

- **Audience:** Who they are

- **Space:** Where you are

- **Idea:** What you are saying

When we think about preparing for a specific talk, message, or story, most people think mostly about the idea (aka what we're going to say). More and more people are focusing on the audience now, which is great. But it's too rare that we spend time thinking about the other pieces, like how can we bring more of ourselves as a speaker to the moment and how can we set up the space to create the kind of environment we want.

One of my favorite examples of this is from a workshop I was leading a few years ago, when I was helping a group of emerging leaders create a story-based pitch for their C-suite leaders. I was teaching them the core concepts of persuasion and storytelling and helping them speak their stories in a more authentic and compelling way.

At one point, we were walking through the SASI concept. I invited the participants to analyze a speaking situation that wasn't going well using a SASI analysis:

1. **Speaker:** Who is the speaker in that context? Are they showing up fully in that moment? Are there stories or experiences they could bring into that moment to help connect to the audience and create a more human resonance and meaning to the idea?

2. **Audience:** Who is the speaker talking to? What does that "audience" know about the speaker's topic? What

don't they know? In what way could the speaker bring their expertise to bear on this particular audience?

3. **Space:** Where are the speaker and their audience? Is that space set up to create an intentional experience? How is the space interacting with and creating the environment and feeling of the experience (even in a virtual context)?

4. **Idea:** What is the idea the speaker is sharing in that speaking moment? Does that idea reflect the insights gained from the speaker, the audience, and the space so it resonates in this particular moment?

One of the women in the workshop raised her hand and said, "I think I know why this one meeting isn't working so well." She went on to tell us about a monthly all-hands meeting her company was holding. The intention of the meeting was to create space for the employees to connect and talk about what was going on.

The room had been set up with circular tables around the space—and the managers would stand along the edges of the room to give employees space to talk with one another. Their intention was to create space for employees to talk without fear of being overheard by their bosses.

But how do you think it *felt* for those employees to be sitting at those tables, knowing their bosses were standing around the edges of the room? A little intimidating? Like they were being watched? Like they were "smaller" or less important?

Clearly, that was not the intention with the setup. But that was the *feeling* it created in the room.

The woman turned to me then and said, "We thought we were giving them space to connect. But I'm afraid we're creating disparity and underlining a sense of inequality."

I asked her, "How would you change things to make sure you're creating the experience you'd like it to be for your employees?"

She thought for a moment, then said, "I'd make sure we have the leaders sit right with the employees and share more of their own struggles to create a stronger sense of community and connection."

YES! And then the following year, when I spoke at their organization again, I heard from this client that she went back and implemented that small change, and it made a significant impact on future meetings as well as the camaraderie and connection at her company.

Walking through a SASI analysis before each time you speak your story can help you make sure that your message is relevant and impactful—and that you don't inadvertently create disconnection when you're trying to do the opposite. It ensures that your *moment* creates the *meaning* you intend.

chapter 20
The Tension of Story Truths

My hope is that you have arrived at this chapter with an idea of a story you're going to tell (or that you're circling around a story by now). Hopefully, you're in the ballpark, because now we're going to look at what levers you can pull to make your story as impactful as it can be.

So let me be clear: ***The story you're thinking about right now is nothing more than a particular moment in your life that you want to create and share with people because it helps illuminate an idea or point you want to make.*** It is not yet created. It is not yet shaped or honed. We're going to do that together!

But to create the most impactful leadership story, it is essential that we understand the ***inner workings of stories***. Because when you know the inner workings of stories, all the different levers you have to pull and adjust will make you a much better storyteller.

Now, even though the tenets of storytelling are highly subjective, there are some truths we need to embrace. Yet these truths sometimes come into conflict with one another. Stories are full of dichotomies and opposites—and they are all true. So, understanding the tension of those truths will help shape and color our approach to our stories.

Truth #1: Good stories are easily followed

The structure of a good story is simple and clear, especially to the audience. And as an audience member, I'm not lost or wondering what's going on.

But a good story can't be too easy or too formulaic. When that happens, our audience starts thinking, *Oh, I know exactly how this is going to turn out. Blah, blah, blah.* And they stop listening deeply. So, a good story needs to be simple, but not too simple.

Truth #2: Good stories recognize rules

As the audience, we have a sense of what the rules are in the world. There are rules around context. There are general rules about how a character may behave in a certain circumstance, given who they are and their role in that world. There are also rules in the world of our story that our characters generally need to recognize (or intentionally break, which still means they recognize those rules).

But at the same time, ***our stories can break rules that don't serve them.*** And sometimes, the best stories surprise us like that.

Truth #3: Good stories are risky

Good stories bring us to the edges. They challenge us as story-tellers *and* as audience members.

But good stories cannot be so risky that the audience starts to worry. There is a point when it flips beyond risk, and it's important that we know where that point is so that we don't cross it. When our audience worries about us as a speaker, or they worry too much about the character in the story, they may be taken out of the story and start analyzing us as a speaker instead.

Truth #4: Good stories are simple

Good stories are clear and concise. They take complex ideas and simplify them for us so that we can easily understand them.

But good stories can't be simplistic. We can't dumb a story down so much that we don't regard the complexity of human nature, or that we come off as condescending to our audience. Good stories reflect the gray areas of who we are as human beings. They cannot be too black-and-white, or the audience may feel like they're being sold something.

Truth #5: Good stories move the audience without pushing them

Good stories invite a challenge, as well as a sense of growth. They show us a different way to be, or a different way of seeing things.

But we can't push our ideas onto our audience. There is a balance to the pushing. If the challenge goes too far, the audience will become defensive and stop listening (and start arguing with us in their heads).

Truth #6: Good stories are specific

Good stories bring details to life and help an audience member "see" the scene in their head. The more specific to the moment and the person, the easier it is for the audience to see it. (All of these visuals help trigger the brain-friendly magic of stories!)

But good stories also have to be universal. They are about you as an individual, but they have to be about *all of us* at the same time. They've got to cover both parties. It is our job to find the universal theme that underlies our specific stories, or we risk losing the resonance and empathy that stories can provide.

It's all—and none

So, good stories are easily followed, but they are not too easy. They've got to recognize rules—and break the rules that don't serve them. They've got to be risky, but not so risky that the audience worries about us. They've got to be simple, but not too simplistic. They've got to move an audience without pushing them. And they've got to be specific and universal at the same time.

Navigating these truths makes storytelling an art, not a science. It's what makes stories a worthwhile challenge that is often dependent on the specific moment we're in. And I promise that the more you play with these truths in how they live in the moment and in your body, the more you will ensure that your stories are impactful and engaging.

chapter 21

Characteristics of a Good Story

Storytelling isn't talking about something.
*It **is** something.*
— SALLY Z

What makes a good story? That's a great question—and a subjective one! So I'm going to narrow our focus to five characteristics. If we brainstorm together, I'm sure we could come up with way more than five (and we might even debate some of these). But I want to offer these five for you right now.

Characteristic #1: STORIES EXIST IN ONE SPECIFIC MOMENT

Specificity is critical in good storytelling. In other words, a good story is not a generic summary. When we enter into one specific moment, it helps the audience "see" the scene play out in their heads, which ignites the powerful mirror neurons in the brain.

When I shared my scuba diving story, my hope was that you would "see" it happening in your brain. Building that visual imagery from the specific details makes imagining it so much more possible. When we do this, it ignites the mirror neurons in our brain and creates what I call an **imaginative connection**. The moment when an audience member starts to see your story in their head? That is *connection*, and this will make it much more likely that the audience will remember your story—and the point you are working so hard to make clear.

There are a lot of really interesting studies about the brain, memory, and story. Because story is so brain-friendly, it sparks all kinds of different and powerful activity in the brain. I am not a neuroscientist, but I interviewed neuroscientist Carmen Simon on the *This Moved Me* podcast, and she had some powerful advice on how to make our talks more memorable.

The stories you remember are in visual images so that your visual imagination comes alive through the specifics in one moment. That connection is the basis for a personal relationship with the audience.

For instance, if I talk about being a first grader, chasing my friend Matt around the playground, stomping through the crunchy pebbles, throwing myself on the tire swing, and scrambling up the slide, all while Ms. Judy was blowing her whistle at us to slow down, **what do you see in your head?** My guess is, you're seeing *your* elementary school playground. Maybe you're hearing how the pebbles sounded underneath your feet. Maybe you're even imagining an adult who might have been in your life at that time, blowing their whistle.

When we put the story into one specific moment—and we bring that moment to life with lots of specific details—that story is cocreated with the audience! It makes the story come alive.

Characteristic #2: GREAT STORIES CREATE CONNECTION—and perfection kills that connection

The more specific you are,
the more relatable you are.

—— JANEANE GAROFALO

If you are familiar with my podcast, *This Moved Me*, you know I talk a lot about connection. Connection is the way we move our audiences. And connection is only possible when we can show up fully, as our imperfect and authentic selves.

From an audience perspective, authenticity feels like, *I see you. I know you. I have a sense of who you are. And your human experience connects to MY human experience.* When we can create that authentic connection—human to human—we can break through that apathy that sometimes exists between audience and speaker.

Take, for example, Robert Kelly, a professor and expert on North Korea. He was being interviewed for the BBC, which was an objectively big moment for him (or anyone!). In the middle of this big interview, his daughter comes stomping into the room. (The joys of working from home—and this was pre-pandemic! Now we all live in this reality way more than when this happened to Robert.)

(To watch this amazing scene in action, check out the video in the Speaking Story Toolkit at the end of this section.)

Watching your kids stomp their way into your very credible and serious BBC moment could be a career-ending moment. Instead, Robert's daughter taking the spotlight for a moment turned this expert (who we might admire and appreciate intellectually) into this fully dimensional person who has a daughter—and whose daughter doesn't always follow the rules but is highly entertaining (and oh so relatable). There's a *life* behind the expert! All of a sudden, Robert became a human being. I would never have cared a moment about that interview; but now I care about Robert Kelly and his precocious toddler who stormed her way into this serious, credibility-building, high-stakes moment.

And I love how the world responded. It was another example that shows how, even above admiration, **we want to be connected**. We want to be humans to one another.

If you are wondering about the impact this toddler moment had on Robert Kelly's career, he wondered the same thing. In an interview with *The Guardian* about a year after his fateful foible, he said, "We both [he and his wife] assumed that was the end of my career as a talking head. I thought I'd blown it in front of the whole world." (I can only imagine. I feel that way sometimes when my dog barks in the middle of a Facebook Live for twelve people.) And yet, the interview requests kept coming. Even more importantly, the requests came with excitement—and good-natured reminders from the segment producer for him to "lock his door." They wanted to hear from the expert with the very real life behind the brain.

I can tell you that when I think of an expert on North Korea, I think of Robert Kelly. (And did I even *know* of an expert on North Korea before this? No.)

Your credibility isn't built on perfection. It's built on connection. Our real, human selves create that connection. Plus, it makes for a much more memorable story! So remember that your mistakes—your humanness—are what connect us.

Characteristic #3: GREAT STORIES ARE CRAFTED

Great stories don't happen by winging it. When you watch the masterful storytellers and they seem to be so "in the moment," it's because they have practiced it so much that they can be fully present—and NOT because they are creating in the moment.

Real authenticity and that wonderful, present feeling of being ourselves fully in the moment don't happen easily or automatically. They happen with practice.

The masterful storytellers have crafted their stories. We need to do the same thing. This means taking the time to think intentionally about where you're going with the story and where you're taking the audience. It means being disciplined in your approach and thoughtfully editing your content. We want to intentionally create moments, levels, and powerful points. We *craft*, we don't just write—and then we open up and go for it in the moment.

When I worked at the youth organization, we would spend years crafting a story and its talk. Most of us don't have that kind of luxury—or that kind of time. But you could, and you can. What it allowed me to do is get into the nuances of every moment of my and my speakers' stories and how to craft and create those experiences. (It's probably overkill for most of us. But it was our job, so that was what we did. Lucky us! It was a masterclass in storytelling techniques and strategy.)

Most of us *under-craft* our stories and underappreciate the powerful role of editing. Editing is a discipline. It allows us to hone our voice and intentionally create an experience for our audience members. Our stories can take people on a journey if we are intentional about the journey we're taking them on.

Characteristic #4: GREAT STORIES ARE RELIVED IN THE MOMENT

Have you ever experienced a story where it felt like it was happening in front of you, and you could *see* the scene?

Whenever I think about this question, I think back to one of the most watched TED Talks of all time: Jill Bolte Taylor's "My Stroke of Insight," which is about living through (and observing) her own stroke as a neuroscientist who studies strokes. Watching her relive that moment step by step onstage is incredibly moving. Even though I watched that talk over a decade ago, I can visually remember certain moments from that experience. I wasn't there, but it almost feels like I was.

Maybe you've experienced a moment like that as an audience member. You saw the person who was retelling the story experience it again in some small way. (Not so much that you start to worry about the person, but they manage to put themselves back into the moment enough that it feels real.) When we as speakers can bring the moment alive and it feels almost as if it is happening in front of us, *it fast-tracks the imaginative connection*. It sparks pathos. If you as the speaker feel it, that helps the audience feel it, too. (You can't expect them to feel excited about something if you can't feel excited about it, either!)

When you relive the experience (even in some small way) as a speaker, it turns on the brain's storytelling superjuice. It creates empathy, pathos, mirroring, and resonance.

PRO TIP

As with all things, be thoughtful about your boundaries. The world doesn't automatically get access to all your pain and every moment of your life. Each context and audience deserves a different level from you. Consider your own sense of safety as your top priority, then determine what level of reliving you can bring into the moment. As Brené Brown once said, we share from our scars, not our scabs. But when you have gotten to a place of scars—and you, as a speaker, can live in that moment together with your audience—it can be transformative for both you and the audience when you share it.

Two Simple Strategies to Make Your Story Come Alive in the Moment

One of the fastest ways you can create emotion and make the story feel like it's happening in the moment is to *use dialogue*. Dialogue is a powerful way to help your story come to life. It is like a superhighway to empathy, to specificity, to reliving the moment, and to emotion—and it doesn't take much. One line of dialogue can bring a story to life and shift it from abstract to alive.

The second strategy to help a story come alive is to *use the present tense instead of the past tense*. This simple shift helps the story feel as if it is happening now, versus a retelling of something that happened in the past. When you slip into the present tense in the middle of your story, it's magic. All of a sudden, it's like it's really happening, right there in front of you.

CHARACTERISTIC #5: GREAT STORIES REVEAL THE HARM

What I mean by this is, *What's at stake in the story?* Great stories create drama. Sometimes people don't want to think about it in the negative. So if you'd prefer, make it about *the positive possibility*. Why does this matter? If what's at stake or why it matters isn't in your story, the story will lack a sense of engagement.

I once heard Nick Morgan from Public Words speak, and he said something that articulates this well. He said that if our audience doesn't learn within the first moments why this is more important than their current greatest worry, they will not be fully with us. This makes sense. We have a limited supply of energy and attention to give; and as busy humans, there are only so many things we can worry about and give our attention to. So if you can't reveal the harm and what's truly at stake in your story, you will lose the attention of your audience. (This is where the meaning part of your story comes into play!)

And truth be told, all of those other characteristics won't matter if you haven't created and revealed the harm.

chapter 22
The Three Dynamics of Story

Your mind is already filled with drop-the-mic-worthy stories. You just have to unlock them.

— Margot Leitman

In this chapter, we'll talk about three dynamics that exist within every story. If it's a story, these dynamics will be in there. But *it's a matter of how much of these dynamics exist* and if we want to turn them up or down based on what the moment calls for. Playing with these dynamics can be the difference between a good story and a great one.

I'm envisioning that you and I are in a sound booth, producing a story for a specific moment. You're telling your story on the mic; and as coproducers, you and I are playing with whether we want to turn up the bass a little bit, bring in a little more reverb, or bump up the backup singers. We're playing with the dynamics.

It's the same thing with your stories. There are key elements we can play with to help create a truly unique, powerful, emotive experience for your audience, based on the context and moment you're in. This is where you get to become the producer of your own story!

There are three dynamics in stories I want to highlight: character, relationship, and change.

Dynamic #1: CHARACTER

Where there is perfection, there is no story to tell.

— BEN OKRI

This seems obvious. Every story has a character—or maybe several! And it's likely that, as the speaker, you are a character in your stories. Sometimes you're telling someone else's story, so your character might be the sidekick or a witness to the protagonist. Whoever the protagonist may be, something is happening to someone. That's the character! And how we develop the characters in your stories is an important dynamic.

But there's another character who is speaking in this moment with this particular audience—and that is YOU. Not the character in the story, but YOU as the character of the speaker!

When you walk into the room, you are a character in the story of this moment, as well as the story of this talk. This includes who you are and how you bring yourself fully to that moment. That's why we talk about what you're going to wear when you speak—because it's part of the character you're playing. We also talk about how you hold yourself, how you walk, what confidence looks like, how you really own your space, and how you invite people into that space.

At the risk of sounding a little too theoretical: We are all characters. We are each playing a character in this play of life. We want to be real, authentic, and true to our own internal character—and we want to be clear about who we are as a character to others so that people understand who we are from the first moment. In other words, how you bring yourself and your voice into that moment with that audience is character.

What's underneath all of my work with my speakers is, of course, a push toward revealing a little bit more of who we are. My belief is that when we do this, we move our audience. Playing with this dynamic means that we focus on clarifying not just the character in our *story*, but also the character of *who we are*—as a speaker, as a storyteller, as a leader.

Please Do Not Be a Perfect Character

A little nudge here: ***Make sure that you do not fall for perfection.*** You do not have to be a perfect character as a speaker—and your stories do not require perfect characters for them to be impactful. In fact, perfect characters are boring. They're unrelatable. They're uninspiring. And they create a glaring and dangerous gap between you (as a speaker) and your audience.

One of the most common mantras I use in my work is, "Perfection kills connection—and connection is the point." Perfection kills the connection we're trying to establish between you and your audience. Don't fall for wanting to tie up your story perfectly. Don't fall for having it all work out. Don't fall for the storybook ending—because it's a telltale sign that your story isn't quite real.

We *feel* authenticity. We feel it in our gut, more than we are convinced of it in our heads. So your audience always knows. And despite what our internal panic tells us, audiences appreciate bravery over perfection. (Think about the last time you were moved by a story. My guess is, it wasn't because it was "perfect." My guess is, you were moved by the speaker's courage and honesty.)

So if you, as an audience member, appreciate authenticity in someone's speaking, why would your audience NOT appreciate yours?

As difficult as it can be to dial down the fear of judgment or our perfectionistic tendencies, don't fall for the desire to polish things and make them perfect. ***It's okay if your story isn't polished or perfect. In fact, it's better that way.*** You won't believe it in the moment. Your every instinct will tell you to reveal a more perfect version because of some idea you've deluded yourself about, that your credibility is on the line and your real self somehow won't live up to the moment. But it's a lie. You, as you are, are all that you need.

(You won't want to believe that. But just trust me on this.)

Who Are You?

This leads us to the question of who you are—and how you reveal yourself in the moment. Simply put, we need to see who you are. From the moment your story starts, what are you (and your characters) like? What makes this story *your story* is how clearly you can define yourself as a character. From the moment you walk out there, it is your chance to define yourself as a character and share who you are, what you think, what you see, what you know, and what you experienced so that your audience can clearly grasp what makes you, you. That's what makes it *your* story.

Dynamic #2: RELATIONSHIP

There are two pieces to this second dynamic. One is the relationship between the characters in the story. The other is the relationship between the character and the audience.

The Relationship(s) between the Characters in the Story

As a way to illustrate this, my husband, Andy, is an improviser. He talks about taking a line of dialogue, putting it between two different characters, and seeing how it reveals itself differently.

For instance, let's take the line "I'm hypnotized by your charm." Imagine that being said between a husband and his wife. Aw, that's kind of sweet, right? What a lovely sentiment, when a husband says that to his wife.

Now, imagine that being said between a grandma and her grandson. That has a really different sweetness to it, doesn't it? What a sweet and tender moment.

Now, imagine that being said between a boss and their employee. Ewww. That's kind of creepy. Just based on the characters and what we understand about the rules of that type of relationship, the feeling of that line changes completely.

We, as storytellers, have to keep in mind the dynamic of relationship—and how we can clue our audience in on those relationships and make the meaning of our words and ideas clear. When the dynamic is clear, it helps us understand the inner workings of what's happening in the story—not just what you're saying, but also what it means.

The Relationship between the Character and the Audience

Sometimes we think the relationship between speaker and audience can be an antagonistic one—or, we're afraid that it may be. The truth is, *your audience wants you to succeed.* And they are open to a connection with you. (And hey, if they're not, there's only so much you can do about that—and thinking they are *not* with you is a pernicious and dangerous mind game that does NOT help you connect with the people in the room who *are* with you.) So it's best to go into the moment believing that they're with you, because that's how you create that connection.

PRO TIP

The relationship with and connection to the audience has nothing to do with what you look like, what your life experiences are, and whether your audience looks the same or has the same life experiences. The relationship between you and your audience has to do with how well you can connect your experience with theirs.

Here's one of the most important questions I ask my speakers before we begin preparing for a particular talk (and building the stories that will connect them): What is the relationship you currently have with this particular audience? And where do you want that relationship to be?

How well does the audience know you? What do they currently believe about you? What are their assumptions and misconceptions? What are the cynics in the room thinking?

And with each new context, you have to rethink and realign the dynamic of your relationship with your audience. Because *your story can change the relationship between you and your audience*.

Dynamic #3: CHANGE

Story is a yearning meeting an obstacle.
— ROBERT OLEN BUTLER

Every good story should have some kind of change that happens in it. It's what I sometimes call "the point of no return," or the moment that changes everything. (If you're not sure what your story's point of no return is, it's likely the reason why you're telling this story in the first place.)

So if we think back to my scuba diving story in chapter 18, the point of no return for me was the moment when the water was rising and rising. It was a vivid moment that changed everything. You might call it the aha moment, or the moment where everything clicked in a different way. That's the point of no return.

Sometimes we've got to dig underneath a few layers to really get to the change. Other times, we've got to meld together a few different moments in a retelling to articulate and make the point of no return clear to our audience. For example, there were a few more things that happened during the scuba diving story. But they weren't relevant, and they buried the point of no return, the key moment I was trying to bring you to. It took a few times of telling it to edit out the things that were getting in the way and keep it focused on that one moment of change.

PRO TIP

If the term "aha moment" isn't helpful for you, think of it as a key change instead. Sometimes that moment doesn't strike us like an *aha*, which is why I sometimes think of it as a point of no return. It's the moment where the drama shifts. It's change.

And still other times, the change isn't about the circumstances changing around us, but about how *we* change.

Take, for example, *It's a Wonderful Life*. In that movie, the world didn't change, but Mr. Bailey sure did. If you've seen it, do you remember the moment when he's on the bridge, about ready to give up? Then the angel comes, and Mr. Bailey is catapulted back into his real life—and he sees it all differently. He changed his perspective. He changed because of the journey he had been on from the point of no return.

There has to be some sort of change, but it doesn't have to be as dramatic as an angel saving you from jumping off a bridge. For any moment of change, it is simply something that happens that changes your perspective—and a perspective change can be absolutely life-changing. Without a perspective change, it's a report, an anecdote, or a summary. And who really cares about that? (Not us!)

Story is ultimately about change. Something (aka the point of no return) happened, and it created change.

chapter 23

Creating Your Story

I'm obsessed with giving the audience something they don't see coming.

— JORDAN PEELE

We are finally there. We're going to lay out the structure of creating your story!

In this chapter, you're going to hear echoes of everything we've talked about throughout the book so far and what it looks like to bring all of the aspects we've covered to life. I'll share the key elements of the structure of a great story and show you some examples from real-life talks so that you can see the structure in action.

But first, we need to start with *why* this story structure works so well. Theoretically, there are a few structural examples out there that I think are illuminating for us as we build our structure together.

Three examples of story structure that work

Example #1: Marshall Ganz and "Me, Us, Now"

First, let's look at this example from Marshall Ganz, a Harvard professor on narrative and social movements. In his work, he's found that stories that shape social movements (aka leadership stories, or stories that create some kind of change) are built on the structure of "Me, Us, Now":

1. **Me:** Your personal story (aka your experience)

2. **Us:** What does your personal story mean for all of us?

3. **Now:** Given the world we live in now, and given the needs we have now, what do we do?

This is an especially powerful framework because it leverages the power of a personal story, connects it to the audience, and pivots it all around what is happening in the current political and social context.

Example #2: Josh Shipp and "Me, We, You"

Josh Shipp is a wonderful speaker I've had the privilege of working with. His structure is "Me, We, You," and he suggests this story structure to help you challenge your audience "without being a jerk."

He starts his structure in the same way as Marshall Ganz, by putting your story at the center:

1. **Me:** Your personal story

2. **We:** Your story universalized to the audience

3. **You:** What YOU can do with the idea

You start by telling your own story, owning up to your part in the challenge or problem. Once you've done that, you can bring everybody else into it without causing them to put up their defenses or creating a dynamic of lecturing or condescension. And once you've admitted your own part in the struggle, it's easier to challenge people in a way that feels helpful so that, ultimately, people might agree with you and act accordingly because of it.

Example #3: My Structure, "Moment, Meaning, Move"
Both of the above structures are powerful and helpful, given the right context. I have always done something similar. This is the language that we're going to use as we talk about structure and story, and it builds on the persuasive framework of "story first" that we've already established:

1. **Moment:** The story

2. **Meaning:** The connection to the audience

3. **Move:** What you want the audience to do with your idea (aka what's next)

As we talked about earlier in the book, the story (or the **moment**) is what pulls the audience in; and what we say *after* that story is really the powerful, important leadership part. It's when we get to make **meaning** and influence the change we want to make.

That's what makes this work different from a story slam, a Moth experience, or entertainment storytelling. What makes this a leadership story is that *you're going to do something with your story.* You're not just going to write a beautiful story and then stand up and speak that moment. You're also following that story up with meaning.

The final element of the structure that is essential to persuasive speaking is **move**, or where we lead people to what's next.

We'll dig deeper into each of these elements later in this chapter. But right now, I realize you may be thinking, *But Sally, how do I actually create this?* That's why I'm here! This is all theoretical until I put it into action.

Don't worry—because that's next!

Sally's STRUCTURE: Element #1—The MOMENT (aka the story)

Let's dig into how you can bring elements of the moment (or story) to life. First, here are some definitions.

Plot

The **plot** is the basic happenings in the story. This happened first, then this, then this, and so on. However, for a plot to be a compelling and changemaking story, it must have more than just a list of happenings.

Most stories go something like this on a very high level:

1. You have a **character** (i.e., the protagonist, someone we're cheering for, or the person whom the story seems to be about).

2. That character faces some kind of **obstacle** (i.e., an issue, challenge, or opportunity).

3. Something **changes** (aka the point of no return). Does it get resolved? Or maybe it gets worse? Who knows! But things can't be the same as they were before.

Inside this plot is where we get to play with all the ingredients we've been talking about: making the story visual, showing the harm, finding a connection to the audience, building your character, establishing the relationships in the story, etc.

NOTE: I've made for you a plot handout that you can download so you can plot out all of the parts we are about to talk through. You can find this link in the "Sparks" section of part 4.

Bringing the Plot to Life

Now, let's talk about how we can turn plot into something a little more tangible.

Step #1: Identify the Point of No Return

Before (yes, before!) you begin creating your story, the first thing you need to do is identify the big moment of change, or the point of no return. When you know what moment you're moving toward (i.e., the moment where everything changes), it helps you filter out what is and isn't needed to get you and the audience there clearly.

When your point of no return is clear, it helps you avoid the "generic" story that doesn't bring us into a specific moment and never seems to go anywhere (or loses people along the way). Those are the stories that can feel like you're talking *about* something, rather than taking us to a specific place or point.

Think about the scuba diving story I shared in chapter 18. The point of no return is the moment when the water's coming up, up, up above my face. That experience—that moment—is what we want to move people toward. It's the moment that people will recognize us empathetically and emotionally, and they will *feel with* the speaker. It's the moment where the audience recognizes the universal experience of being a human facing a scary moment. It's the moment when the insula and mirror neurons are firing—and the audience is remembering their own moments of fear and courage.

So before you can figure out the rest of the plot and what details you do and do not want to include, **we need to know where your story is going.** We're creating the story to move toward that moment.

PRO TIP

If you're having trouble finding the point of no return, think of it this way: **It's likely the reason you decided to share that particular story.** My scuba diving story would have been different (and therefore would have created a different meaning for the audience) if, let's say, I'd had a run-in with a shark. *That* might be my point of no return! But instead, it's about my fear—perfectly embodied by the water going up, up, up over my head.

Step #2: Establish the Character

One of the beautiful things about story is that it allows your audience to get to know you. It's such a powerful source for connection—and you can tell them so much (and convince them of so much!) without actually having to tell them much (or do much convincing).

But a lot of that rests on how we establish the character. This is the moment when you get to define the world of your story—and yourself. This is the moment that makes you . . . well, you. The more honestly and specifically you can reveal yourself in the details of the story, the more clearly we can "see" the character in our heads and connect with them.

How you establish the character tells us a lot about who you are. And it serves a really important purpose in the construction and build-up of the story. The details you choose to include or highlight, which often include the following, tell us a lot about the character:

- What is your perspective?

- What is your life like?

- What do you see or notice?

- What do you take part in? Or ignore?

- What does life look like through your eyes?

Whatever you reveal about yourself in these moments as you establish your character not only tells us about you, it also establishes the reality of the story and the logical reasoning for the plot to continue as it does, building the world of the story in a way that makes sense so that as you bring the audience closer to the point of no return, it makes sense for the experience you want to create.

What kind of character would do the thing you're going to tell us about? If, for example, your character is going to do something risky and you need to emphasize how "out of character" it is, then the details you want to include as you establish your character need to underline what a safety-oriented person they are. And through the details you reveal about the character, you are intentionally building the eventual reveal of the point of no return.

The details you include in the story are important. But maybe even more important are the details you *don't* include! You don't need details that may be true about the character but that don't help you move the story forward and get your audience to the point of no return.

For example, along with being afraid of oceans, I was really into scrapbooking at the time of the scuba diving story. It's a fun tidbit, but it's not needed in the story. (Please know that the scrapbooking adventure went quickly out the door within the next year. Don't judge me.)

So, every piece included in your story needs to be intentional as you move the audience toward the point of no return. This means the following:

- Exclude distracting details.
- Include details that move us toward your point of no return.
- Include details that clearly establish you and your world.

Step #3: Establish the Scene

After you've established the character, you're going to establish the scene. By including specific and intentional details like the following, you're going to paint the picture of where you are so that we can "see" it in our mind's eye:

- What is the context?

- What is happening?

- What was the day like?

- How were you feeling?

- What was going on?

- How does this day differ from other days?

Including these specifics can help the story come to life as a visual image in each audience member's brain—and help them walk toward the point of no return.

Along with moving the story along in an intentional and specific way, establishing the scene with vivid details is essential to "turn on" the persuasive power of story. With each vivid image and detail, you turn on the imaginative connection with your audience—the building blocks of empathy and connection that help the audience remember the story and its meaning. If you include visual details and help them "see" what's happening, you and your audience become cocreators of the story together!

For instance, if I talk about my elementary school playground and describe it a bit as I establish the scene of my elementary crush, Matt, and the daily game of "chase" I played with him (I was fast, but he was faster), I might share with you the railroad ties that held in the crunchy pebbles and always slowed us down and left us dusty . . . or the playground assistant who didn't like us running through and blew her whistle at us . . . or the giant swings where we'd always end up, spending the last joyful minutes seeing if we might "get married" by swinging on the swings at the same pace.

What happens in *your* mind as I share some of these details? Do you think about your elementary school playground? Or a place of childhood wonder and delight? It probably has some elements of my story in it, but it's also *your* playground. *Your* elementary crush. *Your* pebbles, *your* swings, *your* playground assistant's whistle. It becomes a beautiful cocreation that is made possible by a visual scene. And that cocreation helps your audience remember and personalize not only the moment and story, but also its impact on them—the meaning of this story for them.

When I was at a conference for professionals in the presentation industry, I got to hear neuroscientist Carmen Simon speak. Carmen has done lots of research on how to help your audience remember what you've worked so hard to present. And one of the biggest factors is your capability to **create visual images in the minds of your audience.**

Carmen went out into the audience of this conference and asked a man about his first date with his spouse. His answer? "We got ice cream."

"Okay, great," Carmen said. "Tell us more. Where were you? What were you wearing? Set the scene for us a bit."

As an audience member watching this exchange, I can *still* tell you that the man was wearing a bright green shirt and that they were standing against a fence, looking out across a beach. I have a very clear picture in my mind of his first date with his spouse—and this was over five years ago!

Do I know exactly where they were? Or what the exact scene looked like? No. But the image in my head was cocreated with that speaker based on my experience with a fence, a beach, and ice cream. The bright green shirt in my head is very clear, even if it's different from the bright green shirt in reality.

That moment illustrated the incredible power of visual imagery—and the act of cocreating with your audience. Creating the visual image in the minds of your audience is an essential part of memory, connection, and emotional engagement.

PRO TIP

Sometimes establishing the character and the scene overlap to some extent—and that's totally okay! It's not a hard-and-fast rule to have these elements happen chronologically. But generally, we want to know about the *who* (aka the character) before we can fully see the *where* (aka scene).

Step #4: Lay Out the Action

Once you have established the character and the scene, it's time to move the audience through the action that leads them to your point. Think of it as, "This happened. Then this happened. And this happened, too." Each step leads to the next and has a purpose.

PRO TIP

Look for moments where you can let dialogue come to life in your story. Anytime you can put actual words in people's mouths lights up the imagination, and we experience the moment almost as if we were there. That character now comes alive.

Step #5: Zero in on the Point of No Return

Remember that the point of no return is the aha moment, the place where things change. In the scuba diving story in chapter 18, this was the moment when I was in the water, and I was freaking out.

PRO TIP

Slow the story down here. You're going to treat your point of no return almost like it's a slow-motion moment. Slowing down lets the audience know that this is an important moment. It also gives us a chance to pull people in and find all those little details to share. People underutilize the slowdown, so don't be afraid of leaning into this moment and taking your time. It may seem a little dramatic when you first play with slowing down, but if you can be deliberate about it, it can really help your audience become engaged. We are drama creatures, after all!

The Plot in Review

So let's review the plot on a high level: There's a character who faces an obstacle. Something happens, and things are different afterward.

Within that overarching plot (and after you've identified your point of no return), you're going to do the following:

- Establish a character

- Paint the picture of the scene

- Lay out the action

- Zero in on the point of no return

As you do that, you're going to look for moments when you can bring in some dialogue to help bring the story to life.

The truth is, there are a million ways to bring a story to life. I've found that these basic elements give you just enough structure to play with and guidance in crafting something that is likely to engage and tap into the power of storytelling—all without you needing to be a professional storyteller. Sometimes working within a structure actually allows and encourages creativity.

Ultimately, as with all things in speaking, whatever you stand up to say needs to feel right for you and in full integrity so that your voice, your story, your particular approach, and your perspective can be revealed.

All of this is lovely in theory. But what does it really look like when we're up on our feet and in our bodies? Let's take a look at a few examples that show the different ways that this simple structure can come to life.

Example of a Moment

Here's an example of a story that is *not* utilizing the structure of the moment. This is from one of my awesome speakers who was working on becoming a well-known keynote speaker around the topic of resilience.

Here's the BEFORE:

> I'll never forget the feeling of hearing my phone buzzing at 3:37 a.m. on the twentieth of October, 2012. This was another turning point, but one that I never saw coming. One that began with my mom's panicked voice telling me, "Your sister's been in a serious accident," and to pray to God that she would survive.

Let's walk through the structure of this story and see how we can improve it using the steps we covered earlier:

1. **Identify the Point of No Return:** This is clearly an important moment for the speaker. The point of no return is clear: the phone call where she learns that her sister was in a car accident. This is when everything changed for her, and it's the moment she is trying to bring to life. She was sleeping. Her mom called in the middle of the night, saying her sister had been in an accident and that she might die. This story is the emotional core of the entire talk—and there's so much

potential here!

2. **Establish the Character:** In a story this short, is it possible to establish the character? Yes! Every little detail reveals something about you: where you're at, how you're behaving and thinking in the moment, the way the world is from your perspective. As we experience the world from your perspective, we start to connect to a universality within your specific experience, like with the experience of being woken up in the middle of the night because the phone's ringing. That's a universally frightening moment!

3. **Establish the Scene:** We want to paint the picture of the context of the situation. In this example, life is normal—and then it's not. Some details are really going to help this come to life even more.

4. **Lay Out the Action:** We're going to lay out the action next. This happened. Then this happened. And then this happened.

5. **Zero in on the Point of No Return:** Lastly, the plot will bring us slowly to the point of no return so that we can relive this life-altering moment with the speaker.

So when we think about how to improve this story, we want to do a few things:

1. **Slow down the point of no return even more and add more emotive, visual details.**

    This speaker is specific in the sense that it's 3:37 a.m.

But I also want to know what it felt like for her, specifically. What did she experience? What did she see? What did that look and feel like? We need to be brought more into the details of the moment before we can experience it fully with her.

Also, in the "before" version, the speaker slams us with the emotional gut punch fairly quickly, before we've had a chance to get a feel for the panic and worry that always accompany those middle-of-the-night phone calls. We need to create space for the universal and emotive resonance that exists in every story.

2. **Stay in the story with the audience—and don't analyze it too soon.**

Instead of creating the moment and letting us experience it with her, the speaker is telling us about the moment, already analyzing it for us. When she says, "It was a moment that I never saw coming," we don't want to go there quite yet.

So, as the speaker, stay with us in the story, in the present moment. Keep us engaged in the story before stepping outside it to comment on it. Don't tell us the point of the story before the story is done—or else we get pulled out of the moment, instead of reliving it with you.

3. **Use some dialogue.**

This speaker *tells* us that her mom's voice was panicked. Then, she *tells* us what her mom told us, instead of letting her mom's voice actually come alive and tell us. When we hear dialogue, it brings the moment alive in a powerful and tangible way. It triggers the mirror neurons in the brain and allows us to see and hear the story, almost as if we're there ourselves.

Knowing all of this, let's implement some of the changes and see the difference. There are a million ways to do this, but here's one way:

BEFORE:

I'll never forget the feeling of hearing my phone buzzing at 3:37 a.m. on the twentieth of October, 2012. This was another turning point, but one that I never saw coming. One that began with my mom's panicked voice telling me, "Your sister's been in a serious accident," and to pray to God that she would survive.

AFTER:

It was the twentieth of October, 2012. At 3:37 a.m., my phone started buzzing. It's never a good thing when you hear your phone buzz at three in the morning.

Blurry-eyed, I reached across my bed, grasping for the phone, knocking three things off my nightstand. I flipped on the light and sat up, squinting from the brightness.

I finally grabbed the phone—and saw it was my mom.

Oh, no. [This allows us to FEEL the feeling, rather than the speaker just telling us the feeling.]

It was like everything zoomed into focus. My adrenaline started to kick in. I could hear my heart suddenly pounding. It's never a good thing when someone calls at three in the morning.

I hit the button to talk—and heard panic in my mom's voice: "Your sister's been in a serious accident. Pray to God that she survives."

Do you see how those little tweaks from a narrative perspective change the action and our relationship with it? It comes alive. I can hear the speaker's mom in a different way. She shifted from talking about what her mom said to simply *saying what her mom said.* You also get a sense of the stomach-drop moment as the speaker describes how she was grasping for the phone. Some of that language helps us see the story and really envision what was happening.

It's essentially the same moment from the "before" version, but it's coming to life in a really different way. And it's not all that much longer. However, taking the time to establish the character, the scene, and the step-by-step action allows us a chance to be with the speaker in that moment.

Okay, so what's different about the "after" version?

- We slowed the story down and made intentional choices to help set the scene and establish the character.

- We made the story about one specific moment, not about what generally happened—and because of that, the story became more visual.

- We added a moment of dialogue that brought a character and the story to life.

- Instead of telling us about her feelings, the speaker simply felt and expressed them. It became a shared and relived experience.

Even if we took this list of what's different and did it again, we could create a slightly different story, with different elements and moments highlighted. There are so many things we could do in the process of playing with the structure of story to engage and pull people into the moment! This is where you can experiment, share, iterate, and then try again, each time getting clearer and more masterful in your story creation.

Sally's STRUCTURE: Element #2—MEANING (aka connecting to the audience)

Making Your Specific Story Universal

Once you have your moment created, and have earned their rapt attention, it's time to create the meaning for your audience. One of the key strategies for this is to take the specifics of your moment and find the universal theme that connects your story to everyone's story. In other words, it connects you to an audience of people who have not lived your life. They haven't had the same experiences you've had.

How do we do that? Any story can be made universal because every story has a universal, human experience in it (even if the details and circumstances are specific and may be very different from an experience the audience has had). If we lift the hood that's hiding our stories, we can find what I call the **universal emotive truth.**

This is where knowing your audience—and all of their preconceived ideas—can be helpful in finding the places where your experiences might meet. Knowing what ideas they have when they walk in the room—ideas about you, ideas about your topic, and any misconceptions—is helpful fodder for you. Now you have a chance to shape their meaning, understanding, and connection to what you're talking about by experiencing that universal truth with them.

So ask yourself, *"What's the most universal feeling that is UNDERNEATH the circumstances and experiences of the story?"*

Here are some examples of this answer based on stories I've shared so far in this book:

- The universal emotive truth in my scuba diving story (chapter 18) is **fear**. I was afraid of this new thing that I'd never done before.

- The universal emotive truth in my story about John (chapter 1) is **rejection** and **loneliness**. He felt left out and excluded.

- The universal emotive truth in Tanya's struggle (chapter 9) is **self-doubt**. She wasn't sure she could really make good on her speaking dreams and become what she wanted to be.

My scuba diving story isn't really about scuba diving. It's about fear. So when other people hear and experience my story, they recognize that emotion and think about moments from their own life when they've felt that harrowing panic about something they've never done before.

John's story of rejection and loneliness wasn't really about John, his school, or the other students. It was about that universal experience of feeling left out and wondering if anyone really cared. It was about belonging—and not belonging. When an audience hears that story, they will think about times in their life when they felt the sting of exclusion and remember that pain. Once they do, then together we can change that experience in the future.

Tanya's story wasn't really about whether she could become a speaker. It was about her willingness to get vulnerable and step out of the protection of her intellect and expertise. How many times have we all hidden from the more powerful and needed stories because we weren't sure if they were worthy or needed? Or because we were afraid of what others might think or how they might react to them?

We want people to FEEL these stories by tapping into the universal emotive experience in them, which connects our disparate lives and stories together. We are reminded that we're living a shared human experience (as different as we all might be). That is powerful all on its own, but it's also an essential first step in persuasion—because it makes the "harm" and impact more real.

PRO TIP

Once you've identified a universal emotive truth, you need to REVEAL that emotion through the story. Don't say something like, "The universal theme of this story is blah, blah, blah." We need to feel *with* you, not be told *how* to feel. The universal emotive truth needs to be made clear through the story.

It's Your Job to Go to the Audience

Once you know what your universal emotive truth is—and before you can tell people what they need to do with your story—the audience needs to understand *why* they should care about the story and what it has to do with them.

This is your chance to create meaning and shape the audience's thinking and perspective. You've just had a shared experience where they were feeling WITH you—and where you lit up a part of their brain so they could feel a similar feeling while tapping into their own experiences and stories.

So, what are you going to do with that moment? ***It's your job to go to the audience, not to wait for them to come to you.***

If you don't make the effort to connect your experience to theirs and create a new and different shared understanding, your story is a vanity exercise. This isn't about you thinking, *I'm up here, doing this thing, and you come to me and figure it out.* No. It's your job to step into the audience first—metaphorically speaking, of course.

And when you can do that, the audience will understand and think, *Oh, I see why this is important. You not only understand me. You're also leading me. I will follow you.*

Sally's STRUCTURE: Element #3—MOVE (aka what's next?)

We are on to the final part of the structure: **What do we want the audience to do next?** That's a really important question.

In speech circles, we sometimes call this section **commentary**. It moves beyond simply defining the connecting point for your audience and ensuring they feel connected to what you're talking about. Here is where you bring in your leadership perspective and where you lead the audience to a new way of thinking, being, and doing.

When I was trained as a speaker, I was lucky enough to be taught by some of the best coaches in the country. Pam Cady Wycoff and Joe Wycoff created a methodology of persuasive speaking that has won their schools (including mine) numerous national awards based on their approach. Unsurprisingly, when I went to grad school to study persuasion, their approach mirrored the persuasive theories that exist *and* what I had seen work practically speaking in my years of speaking to teenagers and then to adult audiences, as both a speaker and a speaking coach.

In the Wycoffs' approach, they would often call this part of the talk or story the **just talk.** It was a chance to really sink into your own perspective, commentary, and ideas, and to articulate why this really matters—not just to the audience, but to you personally. To all of us.

This section taps into something aspirational. It's not a rant, though it is a moment to let your passion fly a bit. Let's see your real feelings.

Now, why is this so important? This is the part of the story where you're speaking from the heart. We used to say, "Just talk from the heart." This involves perspective, leadership, passion, and insight. *This is the way forward—and this is why.*

Listen, not all of the moments we are bringing to life need that kind of passion and drama. But this is the moment when what's at stake, why it matters, and what we need to do now must be crystal clear. And when a speaker does the Move section of this framework well, it's a telltale sign of a powerful, impactful leader.

Sparks—Part 4: How to Create Your Leadership Story SUMMARY

In part 4, we looked at how to craft a persuasive story by deconstructing stories and looking at what makes a good and powerful story. We started by clarifying the idea behind your story so that your point is clear, then identifying some of the key characteristics. We learned a powerful formula for ensuring that your story resonates with the specific context (aka the SASI analysis) and the learned dynamics you can play with as a speaker to make your story more effective and "moving." Finally, we walked through the specific craft and plot elements of a persuasive story: moment, meaning, and move.

EXERCISES
Reflection Questions Before You Start Crafting Your Story

- What is your universal emotive theme? What does it have to do with your audience?

- Why should your audience care?

- What's at stake for the audience if they don't take your idea on and integrate it into their lives?

How to Craft Your Story

If you're ready to craft your story and you want to follow a process, try this simplified approach. Keep in mind that the creative genius often doesn't work with our timeline, so be patient with yourself. The most important thing you can do is to keep taking baby steps. They will still get you there!

Step 1: Draft Your Story

Don't overthink it. Your goal is to get something down on paper, even if it sucks and you hate it (and you probably will hate it). If you hate writing, do it via voice memo. Whatever you need to do to have something to work off of. And once you've drafted your story, if you think it's not quite done, that's okay.

Step 2: Walk Away from Your Story for Twenty-Four Hours

After you create, it's often best to step back and give a little time for your creation to sit before you continue working on it. Oftentimes, after I step away from a story for twenty-four hours, I come back with the next layer of complexity, interest, or ideas. (It also creates discipline to not create at the last minute so that you miss out on the perspective you can bring if you have the time to walk away and come back!)

Step 3: Come Back for the Second Draft

Stop when this draft is 80 percent done ('cause it's never done, and it cannot actually get "done" until it's being spoken out loud in front of other people). Save yourself the time you'll put in to get it from 80 percent to 100 percent. You'll do it more efficiently by fast-forwarding to step 4 once you're at 80 percent.

Step 4: Share Your Story with a Loving Audience

Share it with a colleague, a friend, your loved ones, your spouse—even a pet. Go for it! Keep in mind, though, that this sharing exercise is more about you sharing your story than about getting people's feedback. The goal is to say it out loud, in your body (ideally not sitting down), with an "audience" so that it elevates your practicing to the next level. The audience's main job is to simply be there.

Step 5: Iterate

Whether or not you ask for feedback (and be careful about who you ask for feedback from, and what you really want to hear!), you learned something by doing this exercise. What did you learn? What did your body tell you? What new ideas came to you? What worked? And what didn't?

This is the process: tell it, then iterate, then tell it again, and then iterate again.

Welcome to the constant and ever-evolving art of speaking your story!

TOOLS and RESOURCES

Head over to the *Speaking Story* Tools and Resources Guide to grab your copy of the *Speaking Story* Plot Worksheet so you can craft your powerful and persuasive story. You can also grab a copy of the Assess Your Story Checklist to ensure your story is hitting on the key elements of a persuasive story.

Assess Your Story Checklist

Below is a checklist that will help you assess the story you've identified. No story has it all, and all stories can be adjusted. There are levers we can adjust in all stories to make them better. But this list will give you a good sense of where yours is at.

Is Your Story . . .

- Specific?

- Focused on one moment (i.e., not generic or a summary)?

- Igniting the visual imagination?

- Creating connection?

- Resonating?

- Breaking through the audience wall?

- Humanizing your idea?

- Well-crafted and well-edited?

- Showing different levels?

- Using dialogue?

- Using the past tense or the present tense?

- Revealing some harm or possibility?

- Sharing what's at stake and why it matters?

- Bringing the audience to a significant moment?

You can get these tools and other resources here:

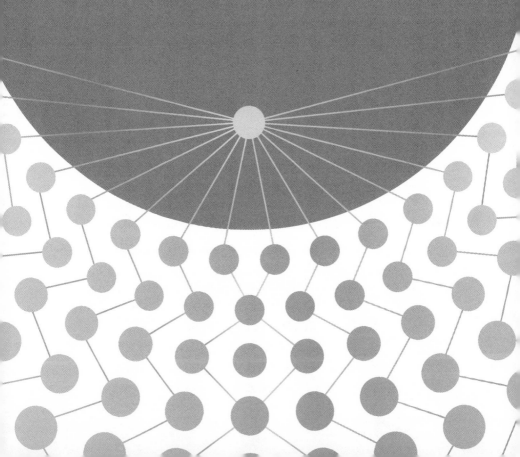

part 5

Examples of Speaking Story

*There is no greater agony than bearing an untold
story inside you.*

— Maya Angelou

In these next few chapters, I'm going to share examples of people's signature stories and how they are using them to catalyze their idea and audience connection using the story structure of "Moment, Meaning, Move." You'll see all kinds of ways that people bring the structure to life. I hope it gets your creative juices going as you think about how to bring your moment to life and create meaning for your audience. And maybe one or more of these speakers will resonate with you in terms of their style, approach, and the way in which they are bringing structure to life in their stories.

chapter 24

Hannah Brencher

This is Hannah's origin story behind her organization and her idea. I chose to include it here because Hannah is more emotively grounded than many TEDx and TED speakers! She's an incredible writer and poet, and she has a very understated approach that is still quite impactful. She is also easy to relate to in many ways. She doesn't have the most perfect speech, and she isn't super "out-there" in terms of her delivery. But she has connected the *moment* and the *meaning* so well, which sets up the need and the *move* behind her business precisely.

If you'd like to watch Hannah's TED Talk, you can find it using the QR code linking to the Speaking Story Toolkit in the upcoming "Sparks" section.

The MOMENT

Let's talk about the moment for a moment. After watching Hannah's TED Talk, did you notice the line that brought it to life?

> I was one of the only kids in college who had a reason to go to the PO box at the end of the day. And that was mainly because my mother has never believed in email and Facebook and texting, or cell phones in general. And so while other kids were BBMing their parents, I was literally waiting by the mailbox to get a letter from home to see how the weekend had gone. . . .

The reason this line brought Hannah's story to life is that it ignited my visual imagination so I could "see" it in my head. Even when I think back to this talk, this is the moment I remember: Hannah, standing at her PO box, waiting for a letter.

If I were coaching Hannah, I might suggest that she be even more specific in her storytelling. I might say, "Tell me about *one time* you were at the PO box. Start this whole thing off by saying something like this." (Please note that I'm just making this up, because I don't know Hannah at all.)

> ***One Thursday, after my last class, I was waiting at the PO box*** to get a letter from my mom. I was one of the only kids in college who had a reason to go to the PO box at the end of the day. And that was mainly because my mother has never believed in email and Facebook . . .

It's very similar, but bringing the story to one specific moment creates a "scene" in my mind. Then it starts the narrative development, including the emotional context that primes the imagination for connection.

The MEANING

Hannah's moment is pretty minimal. Most of her story focuses on the meaning. She got "sucker punched by depression" and moved to New York City, then turned her specific struggle into a universal struggle.

Her specific experience becomes about the following:

- The single mother in Sacramento

- The girl who was bullied in Kansas

- The whole of the internet asking a twenty-two-year-old who "barely knew her own coffee order to give them a reason to wait by the mailbox"

Hannah gives a handful of examples that take her specific experience (i.e., the moment) and turn it into an audience experience (i.e., the meaning).

The MOVE

Hannah's move is really clear: She fuels an organization that is fueled by letters.

chapter 25

Josh Shipp

In chapter 23, we talked about Josh's "Me, We, You" story structure, which we're going to see come alive here. But we're going to see the "Moment, Meaning, Move" structure as well.

If you'd like to watch Josh's TEDx Talk, you can do so using the QR code linking to the Speaking Story Toolkit in the upcoming "Sparks" section.

The MOMENT

What I like about this example is that Josh's story is not his personal story. He's telling somebody else's story, but he found a way to tell it so that it still feels personal.

The MEANING

Josh shares a story about Albert Einstein. We have the meaning when he says, "We've all been there before, right? And before we go thinking badly of that principal . . ." For that connection moment to really be established, Josh has to admit his own shortcomings first. So Josh talks about his son, as well as his own parenting struggles.

Now, the great thing about that part is that Josh invites people into their own failures and frustrations. Simultaneously, he's making people laugh (which is always great, as it's a sign of audience resonance). So even though he's talking about himself, the whole point of the audience connection is resonance. The audience is nodding, thinking, *Yep. I have done that. I've been there.*

The MOVE

Then Josh offers up the move: "What if all those annoyances are actually our kid's greatest talents in disguise?" This is a powerful question that helps us understand what he's asking of *us* as the audience. He's showing us what he wants us to do better, or what to do next.

It's such a thought-provoking question, and it brings his perspective and insight to the forefront. He's not talking at people. Instead, he asks a compelling, clear question.

chapter 26
Jason Jaggard

I've seen Jason speak at the STORY Conference, where we've shared the stage together a few times. The first time I saw him speak, I was in the audience, and I thought, *Holy cow. This guy's amazing.* But what I like about this story example is that Jason has a slightly different style and approach. He's following the structure, but he's doing it in his own way.

If you'd like to watch Jason's talk, you can find it using the QR code for the Speaking Story Toolkit in the upcoming "Sparks" section.

The MOMENT

Did you notice that Jason uses a metaphor at the beginning, instead of a more traditional personal story? A metaphor *is* a story, and it has the same impact on the brain that a traditional story does: It's emotively grounded, it gives us a visual imaginative connection, and it sparks empathy and a deeper sense of meaning.

(Because I'm ABAing here, I'm thinking about what I would suggest if I were coaching a speaker. If I were coaching Jason, I would want to know about one time *he* went to the water park. That would be an even better setup for the metaphor!)

By engaging the audience and asking questions—"What does it do? What was it like? And what is it called?"—Jason is having the same impact on the audience that a story would. This is igniting each audience member's imagination, memories, and experiences. It has a similar structural effect on the brain. And it's how we get an audience to care about what we're talking about.

The MEANING

With his meaning, Jason creates resonance by simply taking that metaphor and asking, "How many of *you* have ever felt like you are moving against the current in this? Or this? Or this? Or this?" That's all it takes. Through that simple question, we come to be a part of this experience. And sometimes that's all you need to do: ask a compelling and resonant question of your audience.

The MOVE

Then Jason shifts to the move by saying, "Underneath the surface of the water, there are jets that are taking you a certain direction, whether you want to go that way or not. . . . Most people try to get you to swim harder. I want to talk about, How do we change the jets? . . . So just for a few minutes, I want to talk about a few jets that unknowingly move our lives in certain directions that usually veer toward mediocrity, apathy, and a life that is less than what we're capable of."

He is using the language of the metaphor to continue the emotional story and connection. We already FEEL it, thanks to the story and the metaphor. But now Jason is creating meaning from that feeling.

PRO TIP

Whenever you are pulling meaning from your moment, use the language of the metaphor and the story to increase your meaning-making! You have already created connection and resonance through the language of the story. Continuing to use it throughout your talk will help deepen the meaning and create even more clarity in your message.

chapter 27
Clint Smith

Clint Smith is an activist, author, and poet. He's a powerful example of how to leverage the power of story to bring people into your idea—even if those people are different from you or have lived very different lives. This short talk was from several years ago, before the racial reckoning that's taken place over the last few years. If we listen to his words now, they have an even more urgent call and meaning. This whole talk is no more than five minutes, but it's a beautiful example of how potent a short, well-told story can be.

If you'd like to watch Clint's TED Talk, you can find it via the QR code linking to the Speaking Story Toolkit in the upcoming "Sparks" section.

The MOMENT

Every time I watch this talk, I'm reminded of how powerful the specific and universal can be. Clint is this kid, playing with his friends. It is a universal moment; any one of us can see ourselves in that situation, playing out there with our friends, embodying that sweet innocence.

There's also the exact contradiction between universality and specificity in what happens when Clint plays outside versus when his white friends do the same thing. It reminds the white people in the audience (like myself) that the world they get to live in isn't the world he gets to live in. The unfairness of it really strikes you.

The MEANING

As Clint shifts into his meaning, he talks to us as parents. He talks to us about kids. And it's rare that a person—regardless of their skin color or life experience or whether they even have kids—cannot relate to that. He leans on the values and empathy of what parents everywhere feel: the need to protect, and the love we have for the kids in our lives. He brings this "issue" into a very personal place.

The MOVE

Clint's move is a beautiful example of a "just talk." If he's determined not to live in a world like that—if he's determined to change the world—then I better be, too.

Here's the critical point: I don't believe that the concept or movement of Black Lives Matter is controversial, but there are some people who feel that way. If we want to change their minds—if we want to get them to listen, consider Clint's point of view, and perhaps shift their thinking—we need to lean on the power of story, like Clint does.

What happens if we don't lean into story in moments like this? Just saying the phrase "Black Lives Matter" might get people's defenses up, and they might not be willing to listen to the value of Clint's ideas and messages. Not everybody in the world is on board yet. Most people will say, "Yes, racial equality is important, but Black Lives Matter feels divisive." (I'm not saying I agree with that. But that reality—or another idea like it—can exist in the mind of any audience, and you need to know that if you want to persuade them into a different way of thinking.)

What Clint's story does is eliminate the controversy of the idea, even if we don't understand what's controversial about it. Through story, Clint is putting the *humanity* of what Black Lives Matter looks like and feels like—and all the moments when that hasn't been true or lived out—back into the equation. That is how you bring people into whatever movement it is that you are trying to create: by finding the *universal feeling* and humanity that exists within our specific stories.

chapter 28
Andy Zimney

This example is one where the setting is a little more "real." Unlike the other examples, there's no production, no "stage," no lighting. It's not a "speaker with a capital *S*" moment. Most of us are speaking day in and day out in much less glamorous situations than the previous examples, and we may find ourselves in a situation like the one that my husband, Andy, was speaking in.

It's not a high-quality video, the sound's not great, and Andy's not mic'd-up. But I want you to take a look at what he's doing here, because he follows the "Moment, Meaning, Move" structure well in a more realistic situation.

If you'd like to watch Andy's talk, you can find it using the QR code linking to the Speaking Story Toolkit in the upcoming "Sparks" section.

The MOMENT

Andy does a classic story: One time, he was in philosophy class, and Professor Wagner asks this question. Then Andy gets a little interaction from the audience. We hear a little dialogue from Professor Wagner. It's a really simple, effective story.

The MEANING

Andy's meaning connection is his own reaction, which mirrors the audience's likely reaction and connection: *Yes, what SHOULD I do today?* He asks a question of the audience, a question that we ask ourselves a lot: "What should I do today?" It takes this simple, seemingly innocuous question and adds more meaning and new perspective to it.

Too often, we rinse and repeat, and we don't make the needed changes. If we want to be more productive and creative, it comes down to that same question: What are we doing with each day?

The MOVE

Andy sets himself up well for the move: together, we're going to tackle that question in a new way so that we can be more productive and creative.

PRO TIP

As you're watching stories and talks—especially thought leadership stories, TEDx Talks, and conference keynotes where leadership stories are taking center stage—see if you can identify the "Moment, Meaning, Move" structure. It will help you bring your own stories to life more intentionally in your speaking.

chapter 29
Jill Bolte Taylor

Our last story is from one of the most famous TED Talks that has ever been shared on the Internet: Jill Bolte Taylor's TED Talk.

If you'd like to watch Jill's talk, you can find it using the QR code linking to the Speaking Story Toolkit in the upcoming "Sparks" section.

The MOMENT

Here is what's especially powerful about Jill's talk: Her story goes moment by moment. We are with her during every moment: left brain, right brain, in and out of consciousness, back and forth. Of her eighteen-minute talk, about sixteen of those minutes are the moment! That's unusual, and I wanted to highlight it because it's so effective and enthralling.

The MEANING

The last three to four minutes of Jill's talk are when she brings it back to the audience so effectively by talking about the universal struggle of feeling disconnected. This universality is what brings us into and creates resonance inside this very unique, specific experience that so very few humans have had!

The MOVE

Jill's move is simply (and beautifully) her wish that we would experience more of the beauty of life that exists outside of our cognitive thinking. It taps into the aspirational side of those "Now what?" moments that we can have as leaders and the opportunity we have to inspire our audience. The question of "Now what?" reminds us that we have the potential to do really big, beautiful things—to dream big with these stories and the impact they can have.

Jill's story has had a huge impact. Millions and millions of people have watched her talk, and it has touched people. That is the gift we have. That is what we get to do as we put together the structure of our stories.

Sparks—Part 5: Examples of Speaking Story SUMMARY

In part 5, we looked at six examples of various ways that the "Moment, Meaning, Move" structure can come to life in people's live speaking story moments. We analyzed various contexts, styles, and approaches, and highlighted each story's moment, meaning, and move.

EXERCISES
Reflection and Journaling Questions

- Whose talk and style most resonated with you?

- What moments do you most remember? Why?

- What realizations did you have about your own approach and what you want to do more of in the future?

TOOLS and RESOURCES

If you grab the Speaking Story Toolkit, you can get links to all of the videos mentioned in part 5; their "Moment, Meaning, Move" time codes; and links to the websites and other information for these amazing speakers.

part 6

How to Bring Your Story to Life

chapter 30
Foundations of Delivery

Good stories surprise us. They make us think and feel. They stick in our minds and help us remember ideas and concepts in a way that a PowerPoint crammed with bar graphics never can.

— SHANE SNOW

It's time to take this idea—whether it's a draft from something that's only been written, or an abstract concept—into a living, breathing story that exists in your body and is shared with an audience.

What does this story look like? What does it sound like? What does it feel like as it lives in our bodies?

I think of this as the "rubber meets the road" moment because (reminder!) **we are not writers**. We may write as a pathway to get up onto our feet, but we are ultimately speakers. The moment when we finally stand up and speak our stories changes everything.

A friend of mine recently lost someone he was really close to. As his family gathered together to tell stories, he wanted to share something, too. Now, it wasn't something he was necessarily nervous about, but he wanted to do right by this person. He wanted to give them a significant moment of recognition, to communicate and express accurately what this person meant to him.

He had an idea of what he wanted to say, but something changed when he took this draft in his head and spoke it out loud. As he told me about it, he described a moment when everybody turned to look at him—and suddenly his words took on a different meaning. They mattered more. The nerves kicked in. All these emotions bubbled up because speaking the words out loud made them real in a different way. It felt raw and real, exposing his tender, bubbling emotions. He felt like he couldn't hide them; they were revealed. He felt vulnerable and seen.

Now, if he had just written those same words down and left it as a note, it would have been a lovely, thoughtful sentiment— and appreciated, I'm sure. But not expressing the words out loud denies a shared experience for everybody in that room. There is something so powerful about speaking words out loud and having those words witnessed by others. It communicates at about twelve different levels, not just one. (That's not scientifically accurate, I'm afraid. But it definitely feels that way!)

In the coming chapters, we're going to get into the mindset, fear management, physical adjustments, and practical strategies we can do to bring our stories to life and physically embody them. And (perhaps a bit ironically) to fully embody our stories while we speak, we have to first work on our mindset.

MINDSET

Many years ago, when I started coaching, all I had was passion and my own experiences of being coached by really amazing coaches. Luckily, I was given some opportunities and found I had a knack for speaking. I was pretty young. I remember being twenty-four or twenty-five and having this realization that I thought was really profound: *Speaking was 50 percent mindset.* At the time, I felt like it was a really bold thing to say to these coworkers who had a lot more life experience than I did: "Hey, now all of these skills we're working on, they're only half of it. But what you're thinking, what you're feeling, what you believe about yourself, what you believe about your audience—everything that exists outside of these skills, they matter, too."

But as I kept coaching, working with skilled professionals, aspiring speakers, CEOs, keynote speakers, entrepreneurs, and other people who, in every respect, had every reason in the world to show up with confidence, they would still show up and say things like this:

- "Yeah, but what if I screw up?"

- "What will they think of me?"

- "What if I look stupid?"

- "What if they don't like this idea?"

- "What if they don't respond the way I want them to?"

- "What if they don't think this is funny or brilliant?"

It didn't matter how experienced, qualified, or totally awesome these people were. It just didn't. Speaking is an incredibly vulnerable thing that taps into our deepest human-ness. So if we are doing it right, it will reveal our deepest fears—fears that, under other circumstances, we have learned to keep at bay.

As my work matured and my coaching conversations became more and more about how to really show up with vulnerability and courage, I realized that 50 percent was too small.

Speaking is 80 percent mindset. In other words, it's 80 percent of what we think, what we believe, what we tell ourselves, and how we show up that day. You can be the most skilled speaker and have the best coaches in the country who help you learn how to move your body and structure your talk and message well. You can absolutely learn all of those things (and they are a really important foundation that ultimately helps you with your mindset). But if your mindset isn't in a good place, the rest doesn't matter. The audience can feel that. We can tell if somebody has really brought their full self to the moment and is doing something that they know matters.

So this 80 percent mindset? It's very closely connected to our capability to show up with authenticity and courage. Everyone I've ever worked with is challenged by mindset in some way or another. It's not like 20 percent of people who are really successful in speaking *aren't* challenged by mindset. That's simply not the case in my experience (even if they don't want us to see that). We *all* struggle with mindset, day in and day out—some days more so than others. We all have to pay attention to our mindset if we're going to embody our stories in a powerful way and show up with our full, free voice.

Creating an 80 Percent Mindset

So, if speaking is 80 percent mindset, how can we create a mindset that encourages us and allows us to show up fully and with confidence?

Tip #1: Know That You Are "Ready Enough"

Let's accept the fact that *we are never really ready.* One of the things that keeps people from really showing up and telling their stories is this feeling of, *Ah, it's not quite ready, and it's not perfect. It's not where I want it to be, I'm nervous about this, it isn't exactly right, etc.*

There's a lot we can't control in speaking our stories—and we've got all kinds of excuses for why we aren't ready. So let's just embrace our unreadiness. We are never really ready—and that's not a bad thing. I honestly think that when the edges are a little rough, it's more engaging and interesting for the audience.

In terms of mindset, I'd rather have us think about being "ready enough." Assuming we've done the necessary prep work, we are ready enough even if we're not totally feeling it. You may never feel "ready" because . . . you're ready for what? It's live theater! So stop and accept that "ready enough" will get you there.

PRO TIP

If you've been following along with this book and creating a story to speak, I hope you'll trust me when I say that, at this point, you are ready enough to put your story on its feet and start sharing it. Remember, speaking is iterative! You won't get better by thinking about doing this. The only way is through. So start now!

Tip #2: Become Friends with Your Fear

Fear is simply a part of public speaking—and NOT a sign of your unreadiness or lack of skill. That statement might put you on pause for a moment, but it's true. The people who speak are those that speak anyway.

So, if we accept and believe that fear is simply a part of speaking, then how do we manage our fear?

There are two kinds of fear that can rule our thinking: **growing fear** and **shrinking fear**. It's important to distinguish between the two because one can be a catalyst (if we allow it to be) and the other can be debilitating.

Growing fear pushes you into discomfort without risking your actual safety. Your body might perceive that you're not safe—and your adrenaline response might be convinced that you are in danger! But you're not in any actual physical danger. Growing fear helps you step into something bigger. It challenges you, and you need that so you can step into what's truly possible as a speaker and storyteller.

And then there is the opposite: shrinking fear, where we get smaller as we do something rather than stepping into a bigger sense of ourselves. This is the fear that does endanger us in some way.

Telling your story, speaking up, or stepping into courage should feel like growing fear. It causes you to think, *This is good for me, even if it's not easy.*

So when *do* we share these stories? If we're not waiting to be 100 percent "ready," and if we're *supposed* to feel fear when we speak, at what point do we follow our fear onto the stage? Do we just do it scared, no matter what?

Well . . . no.

As the brilliant Brené Brown once said, "Share your scars, not your scabs." In other words, it takes time to have perspective on our experiences—and it takes even more time to have the kind of perspective we can shape into something meaningful for an audience (versus telling it for the catharsis and release of simply sharing it).

I remember watching a very famous author take a big stage for the first time. She is an incredible writer, and someone I admire greatly for her courage in investigating her life and her willingness to share all the difficult and beautiful parts of her journey in her poetic, sharp writing. But speaking? That was not her thing. She had made clear on social media—and even in the first minute of her speech—that she was nervous.

In many ways, this was a "growing fear" moment for her. But the story she shared was being shared from her scab, not her scar—and we could feel it.

I watched as the author paced back and forth, hardly ever looking at the audience. Her emotions were raw. We were witness to her first very public sharing of this story. (She had written it down and shared it, but it's quite different to stand up and speak it with witnesses around you!)

Am I proud of her for standing up and speaking her story? Absolutely. But was that moment for me? Or her audience? No. It was an experience for *her*. And that's okay. Those moments can still be important, powerful, and even needed.

But if our goal is to lead *through* our stories, then we have to not just make friends with our fear. We also have to do some internal work and reflection so we can offer something through our stories in service to our audience.

It may take a lot of time before you can share from your scars. But when you do, those scars can be a catalyst and help push you out front. You can feel a sense of mission around your scars and your message because you have been there.

Tip #3: Know That Vulnerability Is Bravery

Vulnerability is one of those things that we know is a good thing. But it still doesn't mean we're going to *be* vulnerable.

I want to acknowledge this: Especially if you aren't someone with systemic power, or if you've been systemically marginalized like many BIPOC, the idea of stepping into vulnerability holds an added level of risk. History has shown us that sometimes a person sharing their vulnerability has been at the very least underappreciated—and, at the worst, has been through something life-threatening. The lesson learned was to protect yourself. In other words, *Don't show any weakness. Don't leave yourself open to criticism. This isn't safe, and for good reason.*

As a white woman, I've been urging people to "be vulnerable" for decades. However, I can't possibly understand how callous that can sound, since I'm someone whose vulnerability doesn't risk safety for me the way it does for other people.

So, as I challenge you to be vulnerable, I want to be clear that **your safety is more important than your vulnerability.** Some people don't get to see your scars and haven't earned the trust of this moment. Some audiences aren't ready for your truth.

But this truth remains: Without some level of vulnerability, we cannot truly lead in transformative ways. So, for the sake of this book, let's assume you are operating within a "growing fear" context and are safe to take these risks (even if it's scary).

The thing about vulnerability is that we admire it in other people. We appreciate other people's courage when they share something real we haven't seen from them before. We recognize their bravery! And it's powerful not just because we are held in higher esteem for our courage, but also because of how that courage translates to the audience.

One of my speakers' keynotes is about mistakes. Every time she shares about the moment she made this huge, public, embarrassing mistake, I see the audience squirm, and I can imagine what they're thinking: *I can't believe she is standing up there, sharing it with us! Why would you relive that?! Why would you share that with us?!* They are in awe of her courage.

And then, as they watch her share from this scar that is

offered up to them as a gift and an example of how we can recover from those mistakes, I see the audience say to themselves (and in their comments and evaluations of her keynote), "You helped me recognize my own need to embrace my mistakes. Thank you!" It's as if they're saying, "Your courage and vulnerability are showing me that I can do that, too."

That's the power of a vulnerable story: It helps the audience feel like they can *also* be brave and do what's needed. Your story shows us the way.

So why is it still so hard? If we know it's powerful, needed, and (generally) appreciated, why are we so convinced that those same benefits will not be extended to us when *we* are vulnerable?

We have to remind ourselves of the exact opposite of the phrases that are likely going through our heads. Instead of the phrases in the left-hand column, you can replace them with the thoughts in the right-hand column and have those on repeat in your head:

Negative Thoughts	Empowering Thoughts
Why am I doing this?!	This is brave.
Who do I think I am?	This is strength.
Who cares about my story?	This is what good leadership looks like.
What will they think of me?	This is how I create change and connect.

I realize I'm making it sound fairly peachy keen and easy. As I've observed over the last twenty-plus years, as we get more and more successful, it can feel more and more difficult to shed the layer of "I've got it all together" to show up fully and imperfectly (because that's what stories require us to do) and to embrace the idea of risk. But as you become more successful, it becomes more and more important that you do exactly that.

We have to fight against the instinct to be the most polished and perfect version that aligns with people's (oftentimes overly rosy) ideas of who we are. I can't tell you how many times, during the hardest moments in my business, people have come up to me and said, "Sally, it looks like you're absolutely killing it!" as a result of my activity on social media and the limited view of my life they get online. But that's not the whole story. It never is.

It's kind of like this beautiful quote from one of my favorite writers, Glennon Doyle. She once said, "We can choose to be perfect and admired—or real and loved. You must decide. If we choose to be perfect and admired, we must send our representatives out to live our lives. If we choose to be real and loved, we must send out our true, tender selves. That's the only way. Because to be loved, we have to be known."

Showing up and being our authentic selves in these "big moments" requires deep courage and conviction. But it doesn't require our comfort. Authenticity doesn't mean comfort. This distinction is important because sometimes people think, *Well, this doesn't feel right.* But **authenticity is supposed to feel like vulnerability.** It's an unlayering versus a polish. It's the edge. It's growing fear.

So authenticity is supposed to be scary. And it's supposed to feel vulnerable. And it's supposed to be uncomfortable.

You may be sarcastically thinking, *Sounds like fun, Sally!* But I promise you that all of this discomfort and fear is worth it—and sometimes we need someone to help us get there.

Tip #4: Get Yourself Pushed off the Ledge

We all need somebody who can push us. Sometimes we can't leap on our own; and if you can't, you've got to find somebody who's going to give you that loving shove. (And if you need that shove, I can be that person for you!)

Whether we leave the ledge on our own or get shoved, we all take the same path. You jump off the cliff, and it could be thrilling—or it could be terrifying! It could be the most freeing seven minutes of your life! Whatever happens, I promise it won't be boring. So let's go for it! Let's take the ride that's been given to you and do our very best to enjoy the leap together.

So find a coach or a community. Find an accountability partner. Find a free group online or a supportive club. Find someone at work or a hype squad of other entrepreneurs who know what you're capable of and won't let you get away with playing small.

Find your cheerleaders because you'll need them. At some point in the journey, you'll wonder what the heck you're doing and if you can really pull this off. You may feel like you don't belong in this big moment, and everyone's about to find out that you're a fraud. You may avoid the hard parts of the process and just cross your fingers that it'll be okay anyway. Maybe you'll even give up (hey, we all do). And that's when you need that loving shove.

As you're standing on the edge of this cliff—and below you is a void of unknowns filled with opportunity—it's easy to imagine the worst. It's easy to assume that gravity is stronger than your ambition and to believe that you'll fall instead of fly.

I can't tell you how many speakers come to me in the metaphorical wings of their lives while the spotlight is right in front of them, awaiting action. They are on the edge of the cliff. We don't know what exactly will happen. We don't know how the audience and world will respond. We don't know if we have what it takes.

And I remind them of this, just like I'm going to remind you of it now: *You have everything you need. Your story matters. And whatever happens, you are brave. And you never know! You just might enjoy it. So go love 'em up—now. :)*

HOW WE SHARE

With the exception of the structural craft of putting together your story (part 4), we've spent the majority of this book talking about the internal stuff: the emotions, the beliefs, the mindsets, and the creative attitudes required to do this brave work.

But when it comes down to actually *doing* the thing, why does all of that matter? Isn't it simply about the skill with which we do it?

Nope. The body (aka the skill) and the mind (aka the thinking and emotions) are inextricably connected together—and they impact each other in profound ways.

What we are thinking in the mind impacts what happens in the body. It informs how we show up onstage, how we use our body, what happens with our voice, and how the content comes alive (or doesn't) in the moment. We cannot separate the body and the mind in speaking. They work together in a powerful, weird way.

I admit that when I first started coaching, I was kind of like, *Oh dear, maybe I need a psychology degree to do this.* I was having deep conversations with my speakers about what was going on INSIDE them way more than I was about their skill and approach. This led to big-time feelings of impostor syndrome: *Who am I to be doing this? What if people figure out that I'm not as good as they think? What if, what if, what if?*

When we master the mindset and combine it with intentional skill-building, that is how we build confidence. Speaking is way more about what's going on up in our heads than it is about anything else, and it's too important for us not to wrestle with it. And it's an essential foundation as we talk about actually getting on our feet and sharing our stories.

This is also where we'll get a bit more tangible. We're going to talk about how to deal with your body (hello, nerves!), how to use your body in space while you speak, and how to prepare for your speaking moments so that you can show up fully, with an open mind, body, and spirit.

chapter 31

Dealing with Nerves and Adrenaline

If you do not tell the truth about yourself, you cannot tell it about other people.

—Virginia Woolf

It was an out-of-body experience.

I've heard this line about a hundred times over the years to describe the first few minutes of someone's speech. It's often how my speakers describe an experience that felt especially high-stakes or nerve-racking. It's that feeling of floating a bit, of not being totally connected to reality. Maybe you're not even sure of what came out of your mouth or what really happened. It's almost like you're watching yourself from above. (And wow! We have so much to say about ourselves as we're watching while speaking to an audience at the same time.) It's a familiar feeling—and that response makes sense, given the research around adrenaline I'm about to share with you.

But it's also not helpful! Being *in* the body is part of how we can be especially present and connected not just to the moment at hand, but also to the audience in front of us.

(We can't really be present with our audience when we're having a simultaneous conversation *with* ourselves *about* ourselves.)

So what's happening there? And why is it such a universal experience?

As you might know, in the deepest and most primitive parts of the human brain is the source of those physical responses. We end up reacting to high-stakes moments (even if they're not actually high-stakes) as if we're in real, actual danger. The part of our ancestors' brains that was yelling, *RUN! LIONS!* is the same one telling you, *RUN! PEOPLE ARE LOOKING AT YOU!*

Which is really not helpful—because the whole point is for people to look at you! So how do we deal with adrenaline when we're speaking? Is it just an unfortunate and unavoidable part of the process? Yes, and no.

For any person who's about to do something they care about—or something they've never done before—it's normal (and expected) that your body will have an adrenaline response to it. How big of a response, though? And how debilitating will it be? The greater the self-trust and belief, the less of an adrenaline response you'll have.

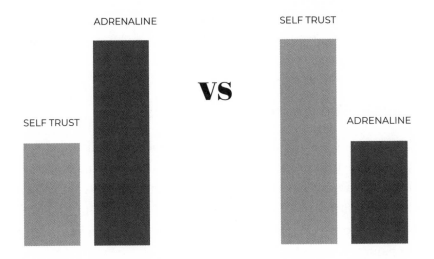

My ultimate goal as a coach is to move you toward self-trust so that you can stand up to speak your story and know that whatever happens, you'll be okay. You can make the most of the experience. (And you just might make some magic!)

So, how does adrenaline show up for you? Everybody's got something! You may get the shakes, a dry mouth, or a trembling voice. You may get really cold (or really hot). Your legs may wiggle a little bit. You may even find yourself doing all kinds of fidgety things that you wouldn't normally do.

For me, I sweat. I always have. My theater-costuming people were always like, "Sally! Find better antiperspirants!" But nothing could stop the flow of sweat, my friends. It has nothing to do with how strong my deodorant is. It is just a pure adrenaline response.

So what is happening? *Why* is it happening? And can we do anything about it?

Let's just say that it's NOT avoidable. It's something that is simply a part of this experience. If that's true, then here's what you can do.

Tip #1: Give yourself three minutes

That's about how long it takes for the body to realize that it's okay. Sometimes it's a little more, or a little less. But if you've ever had a strong adrenaline response, three minutes is about how long it takes for your body to calm a bit and bring your focus back to the present moment instead of bouncing around in panic.

Unfortunately, those first three minutes are really important for the audience! And if you're having an "out-of-body experience" and your body is freaking out at the exact time when you need to be "on," how do you deal with that?

Pay particular attention to—and focus most of your preparation on—the beginning. You might not have total control over what's happening in your body, so you want to feel confident enough about your beginning that you don't leave as much up to chance. (I hesitate to use the word *autopilot* here 'cause that connotes you're not thinking or present at all.) If your brain and body aren't present, we want you to know your beginning so well that you can get through it well enough—which, sometimes, is as good as it gets. So give yourself three minutes, and prepare well for your beginning.

Tip #2: Keep walking into the pack of lions

The more often your body meets the pack of lions and survives (and even thrives), the less of an impact adrenaline will have on you.

Eventually, your body will understand that you're going to be okay and begin to calm itself more quickly. You teach your body that you're going to be okay by simply surviving (and you will survive!). You might not thrive all the time, but you will survive.

There will be days when you're going to have a super strong adrenaline reaction, and there will be days when you won't. It's dependent on your ever-complicated human experience at that time: the struggles you're facing, the context you're walking into, what you ate for breakfast, and whether you slept okay. It all impacts the body!

Tip #3: Find the tricks that work for you

Again, I imagine you may be sarcastically thinking, *Awesome, Sally! So you're saying that no matter what, I'm going to have to deal with my body and its adrenaline issues?*

Yes, it's likely! This response is happening at such a deep place in our brain and body that we cannot outthink it. We cannot mantra our way out of adrenaline. We cannot control it!

But over time, after facing the lions one or ten times, your body will recognize more quickly that you've faced this particular pack of lions before and survived. Until then, find the tricks that work for you. There are some things that can help soothe your body (and your mind) that will trickle down to your adrenaline. For me, whenever I'm hot or my cheeks are getting really red, I hold something cold in my hands like a cup of water, and it helps calm my core temperature a little bit.

Here are some other ideas:

- If you're cold, or if you feel especially jittery or nervous, hold a warm cup that can help soothe those nerves.

- If you get the shakes in your hands or legs, try doing a big shakeout and move the adrenaline so it has a place to go.

- Do lots of deep breathing. This is essential!

PRO TIP

Read *Speaking Up without Freaking Out* by Matt Abrahams. He's a Stanford communications professor, and he's been a guest on *This Moved Me*. In his book, he offers tons of strategies to help people get through their nerves and speak.

Tip #4: Focus from the outside in

We can't outthink adrenaline—or control it by screaming at the mirror "YOU CAN DO THIS" for twenty-four hours straight. But you *can* ease your response by starting from the outside (aka the body) and going in (aka the mind).

Amy Cuddy showed us in her TED Talk that we can convince our mind of things based on what our body does. For instance, if you hold a "Superwoman pose" for two minutes, at the end you feel much more that you can do it.

What we do with our bodies affects how we feel, which can impact our adrenaline response. So try some of these "outside in" tactics:

- Put yourself in an outfit that you feel fabulous in. Suddenly, at the core brain level, you start to believe that you can do this.

- Walk the space that you're going to speak in. You'll visualize it better afterward—and you'll convince yourself that you've already done this well!

- If you need more energy, put on some energetic music and dance. Soon, your body will join you there.

- If you need to calm your body, put on calming music. Plant your feet on the ground, and put your hand over your heart. Feel your heartbeat, and bring your mind to the present moment.

- If your brain is racing when you practice on your feet, try speaking with your feet on the floor. Watch how your brain stops scrambling. (Now you know that the feet and the brain are connected!)

Now, in case you're like, *Listen, lady, I don't freak out!*—that may totally be the case. But despite how strong your adrenaline reaction is, every single one of the above tactics will help you get more focused, present, clear, and confident in what you are about to do.

And if you've never faced adrenaline or nerves before? I have to ask if you're taking enough risks. When I hear that a speaker is *never* nervous, then they're not pushing themselves. Adrenaline is simply a part of the experience of doing something important, real, and risky.

chapter 32
Positive Self-Talk

It's like everyone tells a story about themselves inside their own head. Always. All the time. That story makes you what you are. We build ourselves out of that story.

—PATRICK ROTHFUSS, THE NAME OF THE WIND

So, if we can't talk ourselves out of a powerful adrenaline response, then what's the role of positive self-talk?

Positive self-talk—or mantras, or mindset work—cannot ultimately change the presence of adrenaline. But it changes our relationship with the adrenaline. It turns surviving into THRIVING.

People tell me all the time, "This is all so easy for you to say. You don't get nervous!" Um, YES, I DO. Of course I get nervous! Of course my body starts to freak out. Of course I wonder if I have what it takes.

But here's why it doesn't look that way:

1. My body has learned that I'm okay, so my three minutes is more like thirty seconds.

2. I've been doing this for twenty-plus years, so I've walked into the pack of lions hundreds of times—and I trust that I will survive.

3. I know what strategies to use to help calm my nerves: deep breathing, exercising the morning of a talk, preparing well, and wearing clothes that can deal with my sweating.

4. I work from the outside in: I take care of my body, I practice in my body, and I trust my body (most of the time anyway).

5. Most importantly, I don't see the fear as nerves. I tell myself that it's excitement. That's the power of the mind in helping you speak your story.

The truth is, the part of my body that sees the pack of lions does have a powerful surge. But then my mind comes in and basically says through all of my mantras, *Aw! Look at those friendly kitties!*

The physiological response to fear is the same as the physiological response to excitement. The only difference is in how I perceive it.

*The most impactful thing you can do to deal with your nerves and adrenaline is to **tell yourself a different story about what's happening.***

One of my core values is positivity. I have been accused in my time of being a bit of a Pollyanna. That's fine. But I believe in the power of positive thinking (as long as we're also doing the deep work and not avoiding the tough stuff, which is something I'm always working on).

Simply saying different things to ourselves and expecting them to create different results is . . . well, a little woo-woo. But it's also real. As neuroscience tells us, what we consistently say, think, and do makes pathways in our brains. And the deeper and more traveled those pathways are, the easier they are to believe and click into—for good or for ill.

So the more we tell ourselves things like "You've got this," "They're with you," "This is going to be awesome," "They're excited to hear this," or "I can't wait to share this with them," it starts to make this superhighway in your brain. (The opposite is also true. The more you say to yourself things like "I can't do this," "I'm no good at this," "This will never work," etc., the more you will believe it, and the harder it will be to change that thinking.)

As that superhighway becomes more and more ingrained, it's much easier to access those feelings and beliefs when we need them. What we think impacts how we feel. And how we feel impacts how we show up in the moment.

So what exactly should we be saying to ourselves? Aside from some of my favorites (see two paragraphs above!), there are two important reframes that everybody needs to master so that we are telling ourselves helpful things.

Reframe #1: Instead of saying "I'm nervous," say, "I'm excited"

Of course you're nervous! Nervousness is simply a reflection of how much you care. But the word *nervous* is also negative—and it triggers all kinds of negative reactions within us. So instead, call it what it also is: excitement. They are basically the same thing in terms of how they show up in our bodies, but we feel differently about them. So if we change what we call it, it will change how we feel about it. And that changes how we show up.

So banish "I'm nervous" from your vocabulary. Change it to "I'm excited!" and watch how your feelings about the moment evolve.

Reframe #2: Focus on connection, not perfection

This is worth repeating. Your audience wants to connect with you, and they can only truly connect with the authentic you. (And with the fake, overly polished, and perfected you? Connection doesn't work there.) **This story has meaning for your audience only because it comes from you, your lived experience, and your perspective.** So are we really seeing *you*? If you can show up open, free, and brave, it can change everything. And I mean that.

It's the thing I speak the most about in the world because it is a radical shift for most people. Do you have the courage to reject the idea of perfection and simply walk into the spotlight, open and afraid?

One of the surprising benefits of shifting our focus from perfection to connection is that although it's often more vulnerable and requires more courage, it also lowers the bar and brings speaking down from this pedestal of elitism that is keeping too many of us from truly speaking our stories. It means that we can walk into this moment, take a deep breath, and simply focus on the people in front of us. You can ride the ride that you've been given, whatever happens.

If you can walk in with openness, then your adrenaline will calm down more quickly. Instead of your fear becoming the armor that keeps you from being fully seen and connected, it becomes fuel for that connection. And as that fear shifts into excitement, it can become the energy that connects the speaker and their audience.

chapter 33

Using Our Bodies (aka Distraction Is the Bar)

Stories can conquer fear, you know.
They can make the heart bigger.
—BEN OKRI

It's easy to feel like the body is a bit of a problem in speaking. It often reveals us without our permission. And it's this very personal and visual reflection of who we are, since most of us have a long and complicated history with our bodies. (Understatement of the century, right?)

I was doing a speaking retreat one time with my highest-level speakers. One of those speakers was very nervous about the photos and videos we were taking onstage. Despite her years of experience and industry expertise, her discomfort with her body was palpable:

- She questioned every move she made.

- She was very concerned about what she was wearing.

- She sought out very specific choreography to ease the discomfort.

- She was miserable in the process!

When we finally workshopped our content together, she bravely and vulnerably shared that she did not like her body. I could tell. She wasn't comfortable in her own skin—and you could *see* that.

I said to her (and to everyone in the room, because we *all* struggle with this from time to time), "You don't have to change who you are to belong onstage. You get to bring you with you— and that's all you need to do."

In my TEDx Talk, I referred to Martin Pistorius, a speaker who doesn't have a voice. Here's what I said:

If you haven't already, meet Martin Pistorius. His TED Talk about how his mind came back to life after contracting a brain infection has had over two million views.

Here's the thing: Martin cannot speak.

I watched his talk. He sat in his wheelchair and barely moved—and I was RIVETED.

We all wage battles, wondering whether we have what it takes. But can you imagine if Martin had succumbed to the common myth that runs through *all* of our heads: that, somehow, we don't have something of value to offer people in this way?

We would have missed his story, his wisdom, his *life*—because he wasn't sure if he was a real "speaker" or not.

He is a speaker who cannot speak. So maybe we need to adjust our definition of *speaker*.

Whatever "skills" or qualifications you think you lack, ***you are missing out***. And, more importantly, ***the rest of us are missing out on you***. Because you BELONG on stage, too.

Whatever shape your body is, it's yours. Whatever quirks you have, they're yours. Whatever capabilities or challenges you experience, they're yours. And they're *all* yours to share.

The body is the tool of speaking. It's what differentiates speaking from writing! We EMBODY our stories. Embodying your story means that you are more than a "neck up" speaker, even in this virtual world. In other words, just because they can only see your shoulders, neck, and head doesn't mean you're only speaking with your shoulders, neck, and head.

No. We speak with our full bodies—and we communicate with way more than just the perfect script you have created. We experience a whopping 93 percent of our communication by *how* the script is spoken (55 percent nonverbal, 38 percent tonal). That leaves only 7 percent for the perfect script. Your words live in your body. And having an embodied delivery means that we know how to use our body well.

Here are some key ideas around using your body in your delivery.

Distraction is the bar

Many people come to me worried about what to do with their hands or how they are supposed to move—and they overchoreograph their movements to perfect their delivery.

Let me be clear: ***There is room for you to show up with your mannerisms, your quirks, and your imperfect delivery.*** There's room for you to show up with your natural physical approach, the way that you hold space, and your natural body type. There is room for *you*.

But there will be times when something you're doing in your delivery is not helping you communicate your idea. The only physical adjustments I make happen when one of my speakers is doing something distracting. If a physical movement is distracting to the audience, then they're no longer hearing what you're saying. They're noticing your body instead. They get taken out of the moment, and instead of leaning in, they're sitting back and analyzing. Any analyzing takes your audience out of the experience and puts them into thinking mode—not thinking about your idea, but thinking about you! That's not the goal here.

Ideally, your body is simply a natural extension of your expression, passion, and meaning. When you're fully committed to your message, the body will follow.

Of course, there are things you can do physically with intention to emphasize your point and idea with your movement and body. But too often we overcomplicate this approach and "choreograph" each and every movement—and it ends up looking and feeling unnatural. That unnaturalness becomes a distraction that, once again, takes us out of the moment of the story and into analyzer mode.

Unfortunately, many of us were coached poorly at some point in life, spent time in an unhelpful Toastmasters group, or read one too many ill-informed feedback forms. And then we think that to "speak with a capital S," we have to show up perfect, polished, and overly choreographed. No filler words. No unplanned hand movements. No searching for your perfect word (you should have it memorized). No moving unless you have specifically planned to move. And yet, no standing still! (*sigh*)

There are a lot of "rules" that have come down from some-where on high (who knows where). And truthfully, most of those rules are neutral concepts applied too broadly and without nuance or context. People get one piece of feedback about these speaking "rules"—and voilà! Their hand has been slapped, and they have been warned that a "real" speaker is a perfect physical creature in complete control of their body at all times. So that's what we aim for, forgetting it's not even possible.

Years later, we have some bad habits that we've convinced ourselves are a sign of our professionalism. Breaking out of them requires some gentle self-awareness—and a good coach, colleague, friend, or someone else who can be a positive and clear mirror for us so that we can see ourselves clearly as we grow and develop. (This is not an easy thing to find or offer to ourselves. We do not see ourselves accurately!)

Here's the big myth-buster that sounds too simple to be true, but I promise it is: ***Most of the time, if we just don't think too*** *much about it and simply speak with commitment and passion, the body isn't a problem.* The body becomes a problem when you are in your head and thinking about your body instead of thinking about your audience. And when you hang on to habits that don't serve you (and nobody has helped you steer away from them or even brought your awareness to them in a helpful way), you can make the whole thing more complicated and challenging than it is or needs to be.

Oftentimes I am simply helping my speakers unlearn these habits that aren't even natural—ones they started doing in an effort to be a "speaker," to do it a certain way, to live up to a certain expectation. It's so much simpler than that.

When you're thinking about your delivery, distraction is the only bar worth worrying about. So if it's not distracting, I don't want you to worry about it. Which sounds really easy—easier than I know it is when you're busting through old habits and mindset challenges.

But here's what's important: *If we can let go and commit fully, the movement comes from the body.* When you commit fully, it starts from the inside out. How you feel, the words you find that strike you and articulate a powerful truth, your passion and willingness to be vulnerable—you can see all of that in the body. You can see it in your hands. It even comes out in your knees! It's clear how grounded and engaged you are. When we are committed fully from the inside out, the body cannot help but follow our words and feelings.

And what if you are someone who sometimes thinks, *I don't know what to do with my hands, and I just feel kind of awkward about it?* Instead of choreographing things to do with your hands, think this instead: *How can I bring more belief and passion to what I'm saying? How can I take my commitment level from 50 percent—the place where my hands aren't sure what to do—to a full, 100 percent commitment?*

Focus on what you're saying and how you feel about it. Find a stronger word that sparks a different emotion. Speak to the back of the room. Let your fire out. Because then your body will follow.

When we get our body and mind in sync, we can let go and just do what our body naturally wants to do. Ninety-five percent of the time, that works beautifully.

Now, a big caveat here: **Committing fully does not mean "going big."** It is going to look different for each of us. Finding passion and powerful words that connect with you in a deeper way can happen in all kinds of ways. And so when we think about stretching ourselves into full commitment, not holding back, and really listening to our instincts, we want to use our own scale on that.

A mistake we often make comes when we tell ourselves, "Full commitment looks like this: _____." A better way of thinking about this is, *"For me*, full commitment looks like this: _____." And we can think this knowing that authenticity does not mean comfortable. It means stretching. It means finding our edge. And we've got to keep our own spectrum and scale in mind.

PRO TIP

Our brains and our feet are connected. When you have a wandering brain, guess what happens with your feet? They wander, too. And when we have a focused brain, our body makes more focused choices. If you find yourself with wandering feet, my guess is that your brain is also scrambling a bit. So plant your feet, and notice how your brain gets more focused, too.

chapter 34

Integration

The world isn't just the way it is. It is how we understand it, no? And in understanding something, we bring something to it, no? Doesn't that make life a story?

—Yann Martel, *Life of Pi*

Speaking is not just about what we say; it's also about *how* we say it. Many people think that to do this craft well, you have to memorize your script—and then, magically, you'll deliver it better.

Listen, though. Even trained actors take a big ol' leap from *memorized* to *performing it well*. That leap crosses a much wider gap than most people think.

For her (beautiful and one of my all-time favorite) TED Talk, author Elizabeth Gilbert walked the roads by her house for *six months*, talking out loud while she memorized her speech to really let it sink into her body, mind, and spirit. She was going for something deeper than simply knowing the exact words and saying them in a very specific order. Because saying the same words in a very specific order—and without wavering—is memorization.

Instead, we're going for what Elizabeth Gilbert was going for: **integration**. Integration means that you don't just know the right words in the right order. You know what they mean. You know them in your body. They are a *part* of you, and they have become a part of you.

OFF-BOOK

At the youth organization where I worked for over a decade, I spent years giving the same talk day in and day out. Within about a half dozen times, I had it memorized. I would change it a little bit every time because I was playing with something, getting feedback, or adjusting things. But on the whole, it was memorized. Same words, same order.

It wasn't until the second year that I really understood what *integration* means. I had been giving that talk long enough that I finally really believed what I was saying—and meant it in a different way. I *felt* it in a different way. It was *in me*, in a different way.

It took an entire year. As I look back, one of the reasons why it took so long for me to get to integration with my talk had to do with me as a person. It came down to my maturity and my understanding of what I was really talking about—because it wasn't my content, but rather the organizational content. The ideas had been given to me, and the process of integration can take a little bit longer when you are personalizing content that isn't personal to begin with. It can take a while for you to really believe it, embody it, and integrate it.

But that second year, it felt like a completely different talk. It meant so much more to me. And, unsurprisingly, it was a much more impactful talk at that point.

ON-BOOK

Here's where things can get tricky. Unlike my time speaking to teenagers when I was integrating content I had memorized, you can integrate content that you *don't* have memorized. You might be what we actors call **on-book**, or working from notes, your script, or other helpful "safety nets" (aka not memorized).

What I mean by that is, you've got an outline, slides, or your script in front of you. When I go live in my groups or do a virtual keynote or webinar, I've got Post-it notes on the wall behind the camera, showing me what's happening when and so I can see what's next. I've also got other cues around so that I don't have to do this memorized—and so that I can connect with the audience more. I may be on-book, but I know the content so well that it's integrated.

Integration isn't about doing it perfectly. It's about knowing your content so well that you can let go and be really present with the audience in the moment. It might take a lot of time to get there—or, if you're sharing a story about something that you know really well, you're essentially in your second year of knowing it. It doesn't take much time to get integrated for things that we have lived and experienced, because we've spent all this time knowing it, feeling it, and living it.

Integration beyond memorization

Memorization is basic. I know the right words and the right order, and I'm focused on getting it right. Integration is about why it matters and what it means. It's about speaking more from the body. It is such a powerful shift to let go of the goal of memorization and get to the place where your content is so integrated into who you are that you can show up and let go, bringing yourself fully to the moment and whatever may happen in it.

chapter 35

Using the Stage and the Space

We owe it to each other to tell stories.

—Neil Gaiman

We as speakers spend a lot of time thinking about the words and the content. But we also need to think about the space. The space is how we bring the speaking to life. It's one of the most important elements of your preparation. Anytime you get to speak—whether you're standing around the Thanksgiving table to share a story, in front of your staff, or up on stage to share a moment under the spotlight—how the audience is sitting and where you are in relation to them can change the way the content feels and is experienced in profound ways.

If you were an audience member and you walked into a room set up like each of the following scenarios, what is the space telling you about the experience you're about to have?

This first scenario is passive. The audience listens and learns while you talk.

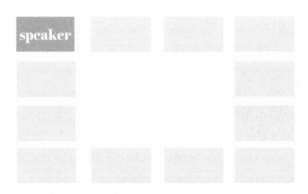

This second scenario is collaborative. You and the audience will all be sharing equally.

In this third scenario, you (the speaker) are leading the audience, who will likely be talking together at the tables.

What about this final scenario, when you and the audience are all one-on-one? What do the space and setup tell you here?

Are you equals? Competitive? Or collaborating?

And in a virtual setting, the space *still* matters! And you can *still* be intentional about how it's set up.

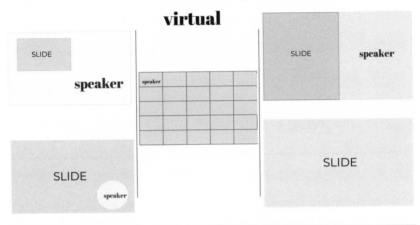

Check out this comparison of three virtual scenarios to see what I mean. How big are you versus your slides? Where are the people who are your audience? Are you the messenger? Or are your slides and/or content delivering your message?

Even beyond how you set up your space, there are many elements that can change the feel of the room and the experience you cultivate:

- Is there a screen? Are slides even necessary?

- How are you going to interact with the audience?

- Will you have a microphone? If so, what kind of microphone?

- How will the tables be set up?

- Do you want discussion at some point? Do you want to encourage (or discourage) interaction between you and the audience? Or between the audience members?

- Where will the sun be shining into the room? How will that affect the temperature in the room?

- At what time are you sharing this story? Will your audience be tired because they just ate lunch?

- Who spoke before you (if at all)? What was their story or content like?

There are a million things that affect space, and all of those elements affect how you deliver your story. It is essential that you find out as much as you can about the space (and all of the elements that happen in and around the space) so that you can intentionally create the kind of experience you want for your audience.

Ideally, you'll want to do a walkthrough of the space (virtual or in-person) beforehand. You need to feel the space so that you can do two things: mentally prepare yourself, and think about the space from your audience's perspective. From there, you can ask yourself, "Is this space creating the kind of experience I want for my audience?"

If something is going to make that experience more difficult, I encourage you to adjust what doesn't work for you. You do not have to accept that the tables are set up in a classroom style (which is my least favorite setup) just because that's how the event planners have set it up. It's okay to be a respectful pain in the butt if it will significantly impact the experience of your audience. ***Do not be afraid of advocating for the experience of the people in the room.***

I love the stage, but that might not resonate with you. We might not be speaking often in the traditional sense of stage. But that may be the dream for you: the dark theater, the spotlight on you, a thousand people applauding . . . (*sigh*) It's pretty great!

Even if you're not going to stand on that kind of stage, thinking about how to *use* a stage like that is helpful in any delivery or performance.

chapter 36
Using Stage Quadrants

The typical stage setup has some language around it that I think is helpful.

AUDIENCE

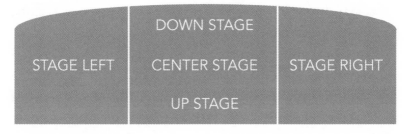

This language and setup come from Shakespearean days when the stage was actually tipped down toward the audience so that the groundlings (the cheap seats on the ground in front of the stage) could see better. Back in Shakespeare's time, there were hundreds of groundlings jammed into the space, while the fancy royals were in the elevated seats around the perimeter.

More importantly, all of these terms are from the perspective of the person on the stage. That's why, as you move toward the audience, it's called going downstage; and as you move left or right, it's from your perspective, not the audience's.

Much like how our space can communicate clues about what the expectations are of the experience, our movement also can speak powerfully (though silently!) about layers of meaning. If you were in an audience and someone moved downstage, what does that mean? What is the speaker communicating to you? Maybe intensity? Or importance?

Your most important message typically happens downstage and in the center. This is metaphorical in many ways. It can be a powerful cue for the audience and helpful for them to understand what you're trying to communicate around this. Because, of course, the opposite is true, right? If I take a step back—*away* from you—what am I communicating? Most likely some emotional distance, along with physical distance. I'm backing away from the idea, making it less important.

Movement also equals change. Oftentimes people may start in center stage. But when there's a new idea, a shift in tone, or a new chapter in your talk, you may intentionally move to indicate that change. Movement can therefore help re-engage a group who's started to drift away.

Any time you move on a stage, you are communicating *something*. And you are not just communicating what you're saying. You are also communicating clues about the meaning *behind* what you're saying, why it matters, and the emotional context of your message. All of these pieces are put together in each audience member's brain to help make a full picture of what your story is really all about.

chapter 37

Intentional Movement

How do we really use the stage intentionally, without being choreographed robots?

I was trained in the speaking world by some of the best coaches in the country. That is not an exaggeration. My high school speech team was (and still is) one of the top ten programs in the country year after year. At my alma mater, there's a Wall of Fame where any student who makes it into a national final round of speaking gets their picture hung. When I was in high school, there were about a dozen of us on there. Now, it's an entire wall. (I'm kind of old, but that's still an incredible accomplishment!)

My high school speech team was formative for me. It taught me skills that I use today and every day. I learned the nuances, finesse, and polish that come from continued practice, precision, and repetition. But I will admit that the speech world can be choreographed at times—partly because it's an artificial situation. There are rules, and you're being judged. It's very formal. And it can be fairly stylized, depending on the category you're speaking in.

I spoke in a few categories during that time: Dramatic Duo, where I'd do a scene from a play with another person; Drama, where I did a scene by myself as multiple characters; and Original Oratory, which is a very formal version of what I do today—an original, persuasive speech around one socially relevant topic.

Let's just say that Speech Sally was way more poised than regular ol' Sally. Speech Sally had her speech ubermemorized. I knew exactly when I was moving and what I was doing with my body. If you had watched me speaking in high school, you would've thought, *Wow, she is so poised.* (I used to hear that a lot.)

Compare that to regular ol' Sally, who was walking down the high school hallway during class one day, reading a hand-written note by her high school boyfriend (again, I'm old) and didn't notice the gate halfway down between sections of the school—and *BAM!* I was flat on my back on the ground with a giant welt on my forehead.

I *learned* how to be formal, poised, and finessed. And those skills can be really useful when the context calls for formal, poised, and finessed.

But honestly? Most of the time when we're speaking, the audience is looking for regular ol' Sally.

It was a process to let go of the formality, precision, and choreography while still taking advantage of the finesse and polish that comes from experience and that level of coaching and expertise. But this entire book has been a nudge for you to be more YOU as you share your story. An encouragement to be courageously and boldly in your body, as it is. A treatise on the power of letting go of what we've always believed speaking to be (aka Speech Sally) and embracing a new kind of speaking: one that is seeking a deeper connection and creation with the audience you're talking to.

I would rather you be messy and real as you speak your story than perfect and polished. Perfect and polished doesn't move your audience. Real (whether messy or not) does.

But we still have these bodies, and we have to learn what to do with them and how to use the space. Which leaves us with this question: How can we be intentional, without becoming Speech Sally (aka a choreographed robot)?

Choreography is very specific (sometimes called **blocking** in the theater world). It's basically, *Do this at this exact time, move here at this moment, and do this with your arms.* (That's what Speech Sally did.)

Ironically, choreographed speakers often look disembodied from their content, almost like they're moving through the motions. But intentionality simply implies, *There are MOMENTS where I'm going to use the stage in a specific way. I'm going to make some choices. I'm going to pay attention to my body. I'm not just going to be unthinking, wandering willy-nilly. I'm going to bring some intention to these moments based on what the important, internally driven moments are—and what is actually happening in the room.*

Let's say you started in downstage center. (That's typically a good place to start.) As you shift into a new part of your story, you want to move away from center stage, maybe to stage right.

AUDIENCE

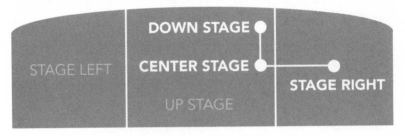

Now, when some people move, because they want to make sure that they're really connected to the audience, they turn their body and walk to stage right but keep their head facing out toward the audience. It's not very natural. I call it "beauty queen walking." Beauty queens are great, but we are not beauty queens. (I mean, we're beautiful, but . . .)

Instead, to be more intentional with your choice but not robotically choreographed, what I want you to do is turn and look at somebody who's sitting at stage right. Then, while you take a few steps, speak directly to that person. Once you've landed in stage right, turn and look out at the whole audience.

The intention comes from directing your energy specifically (rather than in a general direction) and taking directed steps (versus wandering). But it isn't choreographed as in, *Take three steps, turn your body slightly, look at that person for four seconds, and then use your right hand to gesture like so.* (No thanks! Talk about taking the fun out of the moment!)

What you're NOT doing is wandering slowly (or quickly!) around the stage, without intention or thought. You simply want to turn and look in the direction that you're moving toward, pick out somebody to talk to over there (which will help you feel connected, intentional, and grounded), and talk to them while you walk a few steps. Then you turn back out to the audience. You're not wandering. You are making a choice.

If you cannot be intentional, it feels uncommitted. And if you cannot commit to the movement or the gesture—if you cannot commit and be intentional about your space in a specific way—people will not believe what you're saying or follow you in your thinking and in the story. People follow commitment.

chapter 38

Preparation—Get on Your Feet at 80 Percent
(aka Stop Obsessing over Your Content before It's Done)

As we round the corner to the end of this book, we can't just talk about delivery. We also need to talk about how to prepare and practice this delivery!

One of the biggest mistakes I see people make for their speaking is preparing their content or slides and talking through it while sitting down. Even if you end up speaking your story while sitting down, preparing to speak requires you to get on your feet.

We start this by doing a really important strategy that I call **"getting on your feet at 80 percent."** (I'm not talking about the 80 percent mindset. This is a different 80 percent.) This is about stopping you from obsessing over your content when it is 80 percent done and shifting into delivery before you feel ready.

There are some things that we can *only* learn when we get them into our bodies—and the sooner we can learn them, the better. So even if you think the script is perfect and there's nothing you're going to want to change, I guarantee that once you get up and say it out loud and it lives in your body, you're gonna be like, *Oh, that sounds weird.* Or, *Oh my gosh, it's way longer than I thought it was going to be.* Or, *That doesn't make sense now that I say it out loud.*

All these things bubble up only when we let them live in our bodies—which is awesome! It's a magical part of the rehearsal and preparation process. And we want to "get on our feet" sooner rather than later. This will save you time and heartache if you can shift into this part of preparation *before* you finish the content.

Here's the deal. Either you get up onto your feet when it's 80 percent done and then finish it from the information you learn by doing it in your body, or you get up on your feet at what you think is 100 percent and then realize all that time you wasted finessing and finalizing between 80 and 100 percent was for naught because you're going to make all these changes anyway.

So save yourself some time and heartache, and get it into your body faster. We are not writers—we are speakers! Move it into your body sooner so that you can learn what you need to learn. It's kinesthetic learning; and for some people, it's how they figure out things that have been eluding them in the process so far.

Remember, the body is the tool. We have to lean into its wisdom.

chapter 39
The Walk-'n'-Talk and the Stumble-Through

Now I want to share two rehearsal strategies with you that lean into the body's wisdom. Both of these will help you get from 80 percent to close to 100 percent (although, to be fair, you may never quite get to 100 percent!).

THE WALK-'n'-TALK

When you get to 80 percent done (and if you think you might be there but are really afraid you're not, you're probably there), the NEXT thing I want you to do is what I call a Walk-'n'-Talk.

The Walk-'n'-Talk is as simple as it sounds: you're going to walk while you talk out your content. That's it. It doesn't matter WHERE you walk or how you walk. You're not performing this—and you're not supposed to have this integrated at all. You are simply giving your body a chance to connect with and feel these words. We are syncing up your mind and your body.

Does this feel dumb? Sure. (But it's not.) Can it feel pointless? Maybe. (But it's not.) It's just step one in getting to know your content.

THE STUMBLE-THROUGH

Many years ago, I started working with a corporate client who would do these big, high-stakes presentations that were worth millions of dollars. They took this process seriously—and they invested a lot of time and energy into truly transforming their approach to their presentations.

It took us a bit to get there. Sometimes it's hard to change the idea of "this is the way we do it" in corporate culture. And one of the biggest strategies that helped us get there was the Stumble-Through.

My client and I would have these daylong rehearsals. I'd show up to dig in with them, and things had become more "practiced" but not better. Eventually, I asked, "What is happening when I'm not here?" The client told me that to prepare for these "rehearsals," they would spend time practicing. So I said, "I appreciate you wanting to be prepared. But the point of these rehearsals is for *us* to practice together! You're supposed to have it be really bad with me, and *we'll make it great together.*"

The client's practicing in order to show up and impress me at "rehearsal" was just reinforcing and solidifying the habits we were trying to change. They were doing all the bad habits they had brought me in to try and break. I mean, how awesome was this client?! They were trying to do their homework and be prepared, but it was keeping them stuck in old habits.

I realized we needed to rename our coaching session from "rehearsal" to "stumble-through"—because that's exactly what I wanted them to show up and do with me. So as we shifted to our next delivery practice, I said, "As we do this for the first time on your feet, let it be where it's at. It's going to be brutal, and you're going to fall on your face, but we're going to fall on our faces together. I want to be there with you when you fall on your face. I want to help you practice strategies for how to recover from those moments. I want to be there with you when you are working through the bumps so we can help break you from the habits you've formed that are not helping you anymore."

The Stumble-Through is the first time you're putting something on its feet—like, for real. The first time you're putting the script down. Or, the first time you're trying the talk in front of other people. Or, the first time you're doing it with slides or trying it in the space.

It's going to feel stumbly. In fact, we WANT it to feel stumbly! There's so much learning in the stumbling, and we're going to embrace it. Stumbling is great muscle development for handling challenging, real-life scenarios. If we do not embrace the mindset of the Stumble-Through and instead think of our practicing as "rehearsals," we end up wanting to rehearse the *perfect version* of it. Or we avoid the discomfort of practicing at all because it never feels quite ready! We don't ever learn the skills and strategies of being really present and trusting ourselves despite it being uncomfortable or difficult.

I think of it as earning our way to an authentic, grounded delivery. It's a brutal process, I'm not going to lie. There tends to be a lot of swearing in the Stumble-Through! That's a sign you're doing it right. You're laying yourself bare; you're failing and climbing your way through it. In the Stumble-Through, you realize what you don't know well yet. You realize what's not working, and it can feel kind of crappy. But that's okay. That's exactly the kind of muck you want to move through—because this is exactly how you earn integrated, embodied content and delivery. That's how it works.

So get the idea of "rehearsing" out of your mind (at least until you're farther along in the process!). Instead, embrace the concept of the Stumble-Through. Stumble your way through (as painful as it may be), and what you will find is *the freedom to show up and make mistakes.* It'll give you the freedom to play. It will give you the freedom to try all kinds of different things that you wouldn't have tried if you were trying to impress me with a rehearsal. No, thank you. Let's play. Let's discover things. Let's fall on our faces. Let's find your way back up, and it will make you a stronger, more skilled speaker in the end. It won't feel like it in the moment, but I promise you that's where it's going.

Sparks—Part 6: How to Bring Your Story to Life
SUMMARY

In part 6, we explored the relationship between our body and our stories. How do we bring our stories to life in a way that is embodied, authentic, and intentional—and without becoming a robotic, uninspired "speaker"? We started with a focus on the mind, how to let go of most of the body "rules" we have heard about how to speak with impact, and how to use the stage and space in a way that communicates clearly to our audience. And finally, we focused on a few strategies to help us rehearse in ways that lead us to more self-trust so that we can be present and authentic in our delivery and embrace the vulnerable, powerful stance of speaking our stories.

EXERCISES
Reflection Questions

- How is your relationship with your body?

- Where do you feel uncomfortable being seen?

- What makes you feel more confident in your body?

- When was a time when you felt safe and happy in your body?

Mantras

I turn to these mantras to remind myself that it's okay for me to show up as me, with all of my quirks and in the body that I have right now:

- People already don't like me, so I can let go of trying to convince them to like me!

- The audience is already used to me just as I am, even if I'm not.

- I get to take up space and show up as me.

How to Walk-'n'-Talk

1. Grab your script, outline, or whatever will guide you in your content.

2. Walk 'n' talk three times in a row. (There's something magical about doing it three times!)

3. Pay attention to what comes up, like what you forget or leave out. Then, come back and immediately make those adjustments or note them for the future.

PRO TIP

Take your script or outline with you, but don't read directly from it. No one's listening, so allow yourself to talk your way through it. You may discover some new material that is powerful and real—because it came from your body!

TOOLS and RESOURCES

In your Speaking Story Toolkit, you can grab the Five-Day Get on Your Feet Process to help you take your story from script to delivery in five days.

EPILOGUE: SPEAKING MY STORY

Every story has four parts—the beginning, the middle, the almost ending, and the true ending.

—STEPHANIE GARBER, *LEGENDARY*

I was sitting in the front row of a 700-person audience. My heart was pounding, my palms were sweaty, and my giant orange metal water bottle was clanking around under my chair as I kept accidentally kicking it over. I was "nervous-cited," a term coined by my oldest kiddo that perfectly summed up how I was feeling: nervous, but convincing myself that I was really excited. I was keenly aware that I was about to do the thing I teach: speaking my story.

I was awaiting my turn to walk up to the microphone and share a story that was deeply personal to me—a story that most of the people in the room had never heard before, and one that might surprise them.

As you may know after walking with me through this book, I'm an experienced speaker, and I love what I do. I always have— even when I'm nervous, even when I wonder if I have what it takes, and even when it doesn't go well! I have spent the last twenty-plus years speaking and coaching speakers, so this moment should not have been a problem for me. But the nature of this story was so different. I tell personal stories when I speak, of course. But this story felt—and was—different.

This time, I was talking about not what I know or my professional pedigree and expertise, but who I am. Or, more accurately, who I have become—and the changing gender identity of one of my kids.

I flashed to the moment when I submitted the story, my hand pausing on the Send button: *Am I ready for the world to know this about my family? Am I ready to support Rowan publicly—and not just in the privacy of our household? Am I ready to face the rejection that might come with sharing a story like this?*

Rowan had given me permission. Rowan was being brave. So, "ready" or not, this was important. I felt a pull, a small voice of courage in the back of my head: *SEND.*

Two months prior to the event, I was notified that my story had been accepted as a part of a Listen to Your Mother event, an event I'd spoken at and emceed before. It's the warmest and loveliest crowd, and the only place I wanted to share this story for the first time.

The next week after learning I would be in the show, I was with a group of dear entrepreneur friends at a cabin—and I asked if I could share it with them. I could hardly get through the first two minutes without breaking down. Cry-talking was not what I was going for.

How am I going to do this? I asked myself.

Just a few days prior to the big event, in an effort to practice sharing this story without crying, I shared it with some of my speakers in my MoversLAB Program, a mastermind program for speakers who want to scale their speaking for more revenue and impact. It went somewhat better, though it was still unsuccessful: I got to the one critical line and bawled my eyes out. I could hardly see my script thanks to my waterworks.

Something had to shift for me to do this story—this important, powerful, and needed story—justice.

So I did what I tell my speakers to do. I spent much of the week leading up to the event walking 'n' talking the story out loud to shift it to a different place in my body, away from my tight throat and flipped stomach into my grounded legs and knowing lungs. On the day of the talk, I put on something that made me feel good (and brave): my green jacket. That jacket makes me feel bright, bold, and capable.

I left early for the event so that I wasn't stressed. I drank lots of water. I called upon my "cheerleaders" to ask for support and well wishes. And I started telling myself a different story about the evening:

- *I can't wait to share this with the audience.*

- *This story matters.*

- *Rowan is brave—and I can be brave, too.*

- *I can't control what they think, but I can show up with love.*

- *It doesn't need to be perfect. I just want to be present in this moment.*

The truth is that if I never shared this story publicly, it had already moved me to put into words and speak out loud (even to my two private "loving audiences") the experience of being a mom to this remarkable and brave human being. But I wasn't prepared for the experience of that night.

There I was, sitting in an audience of 700 people, waiting for my turn to have 700 witnesses to a story that—up until that moment—had been kept to family and a few close friends. This was me speaking my story: embodying it, being challenged by it, and hoping that it would move both me and my audience.

My name was announced, and I walked up the steep stairs.

As I turned around to face the audience, I took a deep breath, settled myself in front of the microphone, and looked out into the lights, seeking out connection in this room full of other moms (and a few dads). I knew there were likely some people in the room who would not understand or be moved by my story. But I wanted them to hear from this mother about my child. I wanted to speak to all the moms in the room and ask, "Would you do any less?"

I felt the emotion rise in my throat and thought, *Take your time, Sally. Open yourself to the moment. Accept the ride you are about to take. You don't need to be perfect—you just need to be true.*

Through the bright lights, I sought out Andy and the kids, including Rowan. And with one final thought—*This is for you, my sweet and brave Rowan, and for everyone in this room*—I began: "We were visiting my in-laws in San Francisco . . ."

Seven minutes later, as I finished my final line, I looked up and out into the audience, put my shaking hand on my heart, and accepted their applause. As the applause continued, small bunches of people stood up. And then a few more. And a few more.

I don't know how else to describe it, but I felt *held* in that moment. Connected. I allowed myself and my story to be seen— and gratefully, it was. They saw an imperfect story about a sometimes struggling and scared mom, navigating life with her complicated, surprising, and brave kids.

What I felt in that moment was an honoring of my and my family's story—but also a recognition of our *collective* story. The story of loving our kids and allowing them to grow and become their best selves (despite what we might have imagined for them) isn't just my story. It is all of ours. And though it surely didn't move everyone in that audience, it moved some. I know that it moved me.

I'm not always able to summon that same kind of courage and vulnerability. But when I do, I know that it just might be the thing that will move this world of ours.

The same is true for you. You and your story are awaiting a similar moment of recognition and appreciation—and the same kind of connection and change. Not because you'll share it perfectly, and not because you've finessed it just so. But because the audience will recognize our shared human experience in your authentic voice and story.

That's what speaking your story can do. It can move you *and* your audience. And it just might move the world.

If you'd like to read the story I shared above, you can find it using the QR code linking to the Resources section of the Speaking Story Toolkit.

ACKNOWLEDGMENTS

Speaking is a group effort. As I hope I've just explained—a speaker coming into a space to share their story is only one element that creates the experience. It's a cocreation with every individual member of the audience and their tangible and intangible feedback that creates something unique and specific to the moment.

That's how I think of this book. It was cocreated alongside every person in my life at one time or another: every speaker I've ever had the privilege of coaching, every member of my family, every friend. It was cocreated with my trusted advisors in thousands of small and big conversations. It was (very!) slowly birthed and refined and iterated in real time as I was living out these theories—and watching close and brave family members live out their stories in real-time, as well.

So—if you're in my life, you helped me cocreate this book.

Thank you! I'm so grateful.

ABOUT THE AUTHOR

Sally is an award-winning speaker who has spoken to thousands about how they can step out front with more confidence, clarity, authenticity, and courage.

She speaks on the topics of confidence, storytelling, authenticity, persuasion, and speaking techniques.

Sally's mission is to empower big-hearted entrepreneurs and changemakers to move the world with their voice—even if you don't consider yourself a "speaker." (But if you do, she'll show you how to leverage speaking for more impact, authority, and revenue—and be the big deal you are!) She is a TEDx speaker and the host of *This Moved Me*, a podcast in the top 2 percent of shows in the world that focuses on the art of moving your audience. Sally has had the privilege of interviewing some of the biggest names in the industry—including TED Talk Hall of Famers—sharing insights and inspiration with her audience for more than seven years and over 350 episodes.

As a coach and speaker, Sally has worked with a wide array of clients—from names you've heard of (Viacom, Cargill, Paramount, Nickelodeon, Thomson Reuters) to small agencies, entrepreneurs, authors, and creatives who you'll soon hear of.

Sally has spoken in front of thousands of people, coached hundreds of speakers, and been featured in dozens of media as an expert in the field of storytelling, authenticity, confidence, and owning your voice on the many stages we can share it from. But what makes Sally different is how she does it. While most speaker coaches focus on creating more "perfect" presentations, Sally's focus is on bringing human connection back to the front of the room through clear, compelling, authentic, and intentional experiences—because your authentic voice is your superpower . . . if you have the courage to yield it.

" . . . named as the top 3 percent of women in business speakers."
—espeakers.net

"I've spent twenty years speaking from stages around the world, and I've built a global network of storytellers and communicators along the way. Sally's a special kind of magic. I love putting her on stage as a speaker. She's multi-talented and real. Where so many others in this business can often feel a little slimy and salesy, Sally brings a heart-centered approach and connects with authenticity. Book her . . . while you still can."
—Harris III, event producer, entrepreneur, and speaker

"Sally actually makes me WANT to speak in public and present! She is such an amazing presence, her presentation was so insightful and refreshing! Made me feel okay with myself when speaking. First session of the day, and my day is already made!"
—Keynote audience member

"Sally had an outsized impact on the community of presentation professionals who attend our conference. We speak often about the importance of authenticity and then often joke about how people need to learn it and practice it. But Sally simply exudes it; she is just so obviously being herself in front of our audiences. That has been an inspiration to them and makes our jobs easier too. You want to learn how to be authentic? Just watch Sally . . ."
—Rick Altman, event producer of the Presentation Summit